The Fabian So

The Fabian Society has   century
in the development of   left of
centre. Analysing the key challenges facing the UK and the rest of
the industrialised world in a changing society and global economy,
the Society's programme aims to explore the political ideas and the
policy reforms which are defining progressive politics in the 21st
century.

The Society is unique among think tanks in being a democratically-
constituted membership organisation. It is affiliated to the Labour
Party but is editorially and organisationally independent. Through its
publications, seminars and conferences, the Society provides an
arena for open-minded public debate.

Fabian Society
11 Dartmouth Street
London SW1H 9BN
www.fabian-society.org.uk

First published July 2003

ISBN 0 7163 6004 7

British Library Cataloguing in Publication data.
A catalogue record for this book is available from the British Library.

Printed by Crowes complete print, Norwich
Cover photo by PA Photos
Design by Rory Fisher

The Future of the Monarchy

The Fabian Commission on the
Future of the Monarchy

Contents

Preface   1

1   **Introduction**   3
    Aims
    About the report
    A new debate

2   **Britain and its Monarchy**   9
    The roles of the monarchy
    Evolution and symbolism
        Tradition and adaptation
        Ceremony, glamour and public service
    Public attitudes to the monarchy
        Shades of opinion
    Changing Britain
        Devolution
        Cultural diversity

3   **Approaches to Monarchy**   31
    Experience in other European countries
    Debates in the UK
    The Commission's approach
        Principles for reform

4   **The Constitutional Position of the
    Head of State**   46
    Succession
        Abdication and retirement
    Constitutional powers and functions
        The Royal Prerogative powers
        Dissolution and summoning of Parliament
        Appointment of the Prime Minister
        Royal Assent to legislation
        The ceremonial role
    The law
    Conclusion

5   **The Head of State and the Anglican Church   64**
The established Church
  Supreme Governor
  Appointment of bishops
  Church legislation
  The Churches of Scotland, Wales and Ireland
Faith in the UK
Distancing the Church and state
The Accession and the Coronation
  Reforming the Accession and Coronation

6   **The Head of State and the Commonwealth   80**
The Commonwealth and its Head
  The next Head of the Commonwealth
The Queen as Head of other states
  The divisible monarchy
Reform of the rules of succession

7   **The Royal Family and Household   93**
Who are the 'royal family'?
  Roles and duties
  A new settlement
The Royal Household
  Composition and role
  An Office of the Head of State
  Recruitment and employment
  Advice

8   **Finance, Property and Taxation   108**
Paying for the Head of State
  The Civil List
  Grants-in-Aid
  The Duchy of Lancaster and the Privy Purse
  The Duchy of Cornwall
A new settlement
Property and wealth

The Crown Estate and personal properties
The Royal Collection
Gifts
Private income and wealth
Taxation

**9   Conclusions and Summary of
     Recommendations**   **131**
Principles for reform
An agenda for reform
Succession
Constitutional powers and duties
The law
Religion
The Commonwealth
The royal family
The Royal Household
Finance
Property
Taxation
Implementing reform

Appendix A   **147**
Terms of Reference and Members of the Commission

Appendix B   **149**
Evidence to the Commission

Appendix C   **150**
Note by Sir Michael Wheeler-Booth

Preface

The Commission on the Future of the Monarchy was established by the Fabian Society in May 2002. Its ten members, not all of them Fabians or Labour supporters, were selected to bring a range of relevant experience and expertise to the subject. Our terms of reference asked us to 'examine the role and functions of the monarchy and its position within a changing society and constitution', with the aim of making 'recommendations on ways in which the office of head of state can meet the social and political needs of today and the foreseeable future'. We held a series of meetings, spread over twelve months, at which we interviewed expert witnesses and considered research papers written by the Commission Secretariat and other written evidence. This is our final report.

In any country the Head of State is an important institution. Its future is therefore an important topic and deserves serious public debate. There is more to the subject than the dissection of past marriages and speculation about future ones.

On the spectrum of opinions from convinced republicans to fervent monarchists, opposition to change comes from both extremes. The convinced republicans say 'why reform the monarchy? Abolish it, or just leave it to rot.' The fervent monarchists, on the other hand, treat the institution like a Ming vase: it must not be disturbed at all for fear of destroying it. Between these two is a large group – we believe a majority – who would prefer Britain to remain a monarchy, but regard some features of the present constitutional and financial arrangements as indefensible.

The initiative for the Commission did not come from the Government. Its reaction to our report may well be that there are more urgent priorities for reform. In a sense there always are. But the danger of that approach is that the institution will gradually seem more and more anachronistic, and thus less and less acceptable; or that action will one day be forced by a crisis. Those who wish the monarchy well should hesitate before they nail their colours to the mast of the status quo.

We are grateful to all those who submitted evidence and particularly those who took the time to meet the Commission. They are not responsible for the views we express. We are very grateful to the Dartmouth Street Trust for providing financial support for the Commission's research, and to the Fabian Society for its logistical and administrative support. We are particularly appreciative of the excellent work of Adrian Harvey, Deputy General Secretary of the Fabian Society, who acted as Secretary to the Commission and prepared this report. Our thanks also go to Adrian Hughes and Anoushka Alexander, the Commission's industrious researchers. The final report was edited by Ellie Levenson. Editorial assistance was provided by Matthew Walsham and Nathaniel Copsey. Michael Jacobs, Fabian Society General Secretary, provided valuable support to the project throughout.

We are sorry that one of our number, Sir Michael Wheeler-Booth, felt unable to sign the final report. His views are set out in an appendix, where it will be seen that he agrees with many of our specific proposals. The report itself represents the collective view of the other nine Commissioners. We hope that it will generate a vigorous and intelligent debate.

David Bean QC
Chair of the Fabian Commission on the Future of the Monarchy
June 2003

Chapter 1

Introduction

Twenty years ago, a report questioning the future of the monarchy would have been more or less unthinkable. Such was the standing of the monarchy within Britain before the 1980s that a Commission of Inquiry examining its role and structure would have been regarded by many people as, at the very least, grossly impertinent. It is a measure of the changes which have taken place in British society and British public opinion that today it is not this report, but those past attitudes of deference, which now seem remarkable.

In part, this shift has been a result of turbulent times for the royal family. The Queen famously described 1992 as her *annus horribilis*, with royal divorce, two marital breakdowns and the fire at Windsor Castle. But as it turned out this was just the start of a long period of very public difficulties. 1994 saw televised admissions of adultery by both the Prince and Princess of Wales, and thereafter increasing public antagonism between them. In 1997 the unprecedented public reaction to Princess Diana's death, followed by the extraordinary speech made at her funeral by her brother Earl Spencer, led to serious claims that the royal family had become fatally estranged from the British public. That proved unfounded, yet just five years later two separate trials of palace butlers, both stopped in strange circumstances, raised new questions about the royal family and household. The legal position of the monarch, the judgement of both the Queen and the Prince of Wales, and the honesty of some palace staff were all brought into doubt. It was nearly 150 years ago that the constitutional historian Walter Bagehot famously warned that daylight should not be let in on the magic of monarchy. Over the last ten the curtains have been opened, and, as he predicted, the shadows revealed have not enhanced the institution's standing.

Of course, the troubles of the last fifteen years have been far from unrelenting. The success of the Golden Jubilee celebrations of 2002 confounded those who had predicted (partly because of the turbulence of the previous decade) an embarrassing failure. The public reaction to the death of the Queen Mother demonstrated the continued affection and support for the institution felt by many British people, support routinely confirmed by opinion polls.

In fact, personal troubles, and the public reaction to them, are not a new feature of royal experience – individual monarchs and princes have regularly fallen foul of public sentiment. What has changed is British society and culture. In 1952 most Britons believed the new Queen was chosen by God; today few pollsters would even ask the question. Increasingly democratic in its attitudes, Britain is now less deferential and more sceptical – some might say cynical – about authority. No institution, not even the monarchy, escapes the effects.

In part, the Fabian Society's reasons for establishing a Commission on the Future of the Monarchy related to these trends. This is not the first time that the Society has addressed this question. In 1996 its pamphlet *Long to Reign Over Us?* by Paul Richards raised many of the same issues. But the eve of the Jubilee year, when we started to plan the Commission, seemed a particularly opportune moment to consider in greater detail the next 50 years in the development of this central British institution. At that time, we did not know whether the Jubilee celebrations would be successful; and no-one knew the names of palace butlers. But half a century of Elizabeth II's reign seemed a significant point to stop and reflect on how well the monarchy was continuing to serve our changing society.

Of greater importance in setting up the Commission, however, was the position of the monarch in our changing constitution. Since 1997, Britain has undergone the single most significant period of constitutional reform in over a century. A parliament has been restored to Scotland, and assemblies created in Wales and Northern Ireland; all three are elected by proportional vot-

ing systems. The development of democratic regional government in England has begun, with a directly elected mayor and
assembly in London and legislation in place to allow other
regions to follow suit. The right of most hereditary peers to sit in
the House of Lords has been ended after 700 years. The Human
Rights Act has given UK citizens access to European Convention
rights for the first time through domestic courts. The process of
closer integration in the European Union continues, even if its
precise destination remains uncertain. And yet the institution at
the apex of our constitution has remained untouched, and
indeed largely undiscussed. For the Fabian Society it seemed
appropriate to fill this gap: to add the role of the UK's Head of
State to the country's new constitutional debate.

Aims

As given by its terms of reference, the Commission's aim from
the outset was to design an appropriate constitutional and social
role for the Head of State as an essential element of our system
of governance. It was not, primarily, to examine how the holder
of that office should be appointed. So readers will not find in
these pages an extended discussion on the merits or otherwise of
abolition of the monarchy or the creation of a republic. We
believe strongly that these possible futures should be publicly
debated; they are clearly an important part of the constitutional
argument. But they were not our focus. Our aim was to define
the office of Head of State appropriate to modern Britain –
whether that office was filled by a hereditary monarch or an
elected president.

   If we had started with an entirely clean sheet, it is unlikely that
we would have argued for a monarch as Head of State. But neither Britain's history nor its constitution is a clean sheet: it is
impossible simply to ignore the existing system and how, historically, we got to where we are now. Although some of the
Commissioners are republicans and others not, we have all been
struck by the weight of continuing public support for the
monarchy. This tends to make arguments for a republic somewhat academic, at least for the foreseeable future. If there were a

referendum today on the institution's abolition it is pretty safe to say that it would be unsuccessful, which in itself rather undermines the democratic basis of the republican case. The people, it seems, are broadly happy with their monarchy.

Our primary focus was therefore on the office of Head of State. However we were well aware that we would not be able to draw such a tight boundary around the subject. The monarchy pervades many of the other parts of the British constitution and indeed society more widely. The Queen has formal duties beyond the UK. So other, broader questions had to be considered, including the interaction of the monarch with the law, the Church of England and the Commonwealth. As far as possible, however, our attention has been limited to the issues that relate directly to the role of the monarch; we have not sought to answer those questions which primarily relate to the role or structure of other institutions. So, for example, we make recommendations on the relationship between the sovereign and the Anglican Church; but not on other aspects of the establishment of the Church of England.

Similarly, we could not restrict our attention to the dry mechanics of the institution. The monarchy is much more than the duties and powers of the office: it plays an important role in British society and national identity. We discuss these and other symbolic roles, but the report does not consider the personalities or personal lives of members of the royal family. We are only concerned with their public duties.

About the report

The report falls into three parts. The first two chapters are concerned with ways of thinking about monarchy: first socially and historically, and then in terms of the constitution. Chapter 2 outlines the historical development of the institution, the shape of current public attitudes towards it and its symbolic role in a changing society. Chapter 3 describes the political debates about monarchy, and sets out some comparative material on both monarchies and republics in other European countries. The chapter concludes by setting out the principles that underpin the Commission's own arguments and proposals.

The next three chapters consider the formal position of the Head of State. In Chapter 4 the focus is on the constitutional role of the office, especially ways in which its powers and duties are, and should be, defined. The chapter considers the appropriateness of both the current rules of succession and the status of the monarch in relation to the law. Chapter 5 deals with the formal relationship between the Head of State and the Anglican Church, and considers how this might be reformed to reflect better the increasingly diverse religious life of the UK. In Chapter 6 we consider the future relationship of the British monarch with those other Commonwealth countries of which he or she is Head of State, and with the Commonwealth as a whole.

The structure, management and financing of the institution are the subject of the final two chapters. Chapter 7 considers the royal family and royal household – the organisation of Buckingham and St James's Palaces. Chapter 8 then questions how the UK should pay for its Head of State, and examines the questions of property and taxation.

A concluding chapter summarises the principles and arguments of the report as a whole, and lists all the recommendations.

A new debate

Over the year of the Commission's deliberations it has become clear to us that there are many strengths to Britain's constitutional monarchy, but without reform these may decline – possibly quite quickly. Social and cultural change has left Britain, in important ways, a different country from that which existed when Elizabeth II acceded to the throne; and constitutional reform means that the system of which the monarchy is at the heart has been similarly transformed. In a time of such fluidity, the Commission has come to the view that merely preserving the status quo is not a sensible option.

The Future of the Monarchy

We believe it is time for these important questions to be properly and publicly debated. We hope this report will help in that process.

Chapter 2

Britain and its Monarchy

Any debate about the future of the British monarchy needs to start with two simple yet rather profound questions. What exactly is the monarchy and what does it do?

Anyone could be forgiven for not giving these questions much thought. The institution of monarchy has been such a fixed point in British life for so long that it is easy to take for granted its precise function and role. For many people the monarchy no doubt seems like an unchanging feature of the nation's historic landscape, whose existence is almost part of the definition of Britain itself. Indeed, as members of the royal family have over recent years become quasi-celebrities, objects of pervasive attention in tabloid newspapers and magazines, it has often been difficult to recall what their ostensible duties are.

There are in fact two different dimensions to the monarchy, two kinds of role, and it is helpful to distinguish them.

The roles of the monarchy

The first role relates to the monarch's constitutional and institutional functions. These are the powers and duties given to the sovereign within the British constitution, along with the roles which the monarch plays within other institutions – notably the Commonwealth and the Church of England.

Constitutionally, the monarch is the Head of State of the UK. It is commonly believed that this is just a ceremonial position, without any real power. But this view is in important respects mistaken. Some of the monarch's powers as Head of State are quite real, and can be used – indeed they sometimes are. But more than this, the monarchy is the keystone in Britain's unwritten constitution, in many ways its central and founding idea. Its constitutional significance therefore extends beyond the sovereign's own duties.

The UK is a constitutional monarchy. This means that the hereditary monarch provides ultimate legitimacy for state institutions, but the powers of the monarch are constitutionally constrained. Political power is exercised by a democratically elected government. The UK is unusual among European constitutional monarchies in not having a unitary and written constitution to define the relationship between the monarchy and the democratic institutions of government. The constraints placed upon the monarch's powers are determined by a combination of common law, legislation (enacted at different times and in different historical contexts) and convention. Whereas the powers of other constitutional monarchs are legally defined and codified, the UK's monarchy is regulated by custom and practice as much as law. Indeed, as constitutional lawyer Joe Jacob argues in *The Republican Crown*:

'At the heart of Britain, law does not rule. The Crown is at this centre. If there are laws, they are not justiciable in any ordinary sense and not discernible by legal technique. We may grant that the boundaries of this core are defined by law and, certainly that its scope is diminishing; but, in this centre, the rule of law does not operate.' [1]

Formally, democratic government takes place under the authority of the Crown. Parliament is opened by the monarch every year because it is constitutionally her institution; she summons and dissolves it. Though democratically elected, Members of Parliament swear allegiance to the monarch, not – as in other countries – to the constitution, the people, or the nation. So do members of the Armed Forces, police and judges. It is 'Her Majesty's Government', rather than formally the government of the public: this is why the monarch every year gives the Queen's Speech setting out its legislative plans. The monarch is similarly the fount of British law: it is in her name (the Crown versus…) that prosecutions are mounted.

In reality the monarch is rather more subject to the will of Parliament than the formal arrangements suggest. Indeed, *in extremis,* it is the legislature which determines who the monarch will be. As the historian Ben Pimlott has put it:

'In Britain, as every schoolchild knows, the definition of royalty is ultimately, and on occasion directly, in the hands of Parliament. This was made plain in 1688, when Parliament declared that the fleeing James II had, in effect, abdicated. If there was any remaining doubt, it was banished to the profound humiliation of the Windsor dynasty in 1936, when a Prime Minister with the backing of Parliament required Edward VIII to choose between a marriage deemed inappropriate and the throne.' [2]

Nevertheless, it is also true that under the unwritten constitution the monarch retains considerable formal legal powers – collectively termed the Royal Prerogative powers. Many of these – such as the power to make war, to conclude treaties and to recognise foreign states – are effectively exercised by government ministers, and today are not properly thought of as powers of the sovereign at all. But others, such as the power to appoint and dismiss the Prime Minister, to dissolve Parliament and to assent to legislation, still have genuine scope for discretion. In this sense they remain real powers of the sovereign.

Unusually, the British monarch is also Head of State of several other countries. While a majority of members of the British Commonwealth are now republics with elected or otherwise appointed presidents, fifteen nations – among them Australia, Canada, New Zealand, Jamaica and Papua New Guinea – have retained the British monarch as their Head of State. The present Queen also holds the title of, and plays an important role as, Head of the Commonwealth of Nations. However, this is not a constitutional position, and it does not relate to the monarch's status as Head of State of the sixteen countries.

Finally, the monarch is the Supreme Governor of the Church of England, the established church in England. This is a constitutional position derived from Henry VIII's Act of Supremacy in 1559 and formally links the church to the state. The monarch has a less central role in relation to the Church of Scotland, and no role at all in the Anglican churches of Wales and Ireland.

These constitutional and institutional roles are the foundation of the monarchy. We shall discuss them further in Chapter 4. But in many ways they are not the roles which most attract the public's attention. This chapter concentrates on those which do.

The second dimension to monarchy concerns the social and cultural roles which the institution plays within British society. For the monarchy is not just a constitutional structure. It is a symbolic one. More than most public institutions, the monarchy brings with it a range of social and cultural meanings – some which it has sought to represent itself, many projected onto it by the society of which it is a part. As a symbol the monarchy is both powerful and pervasive. It is almost universally recognised: images of the royal family are perhaps more widely seen around the world than those of any other non-executive Head of State. And in being seen, monarchy cannot help but say something about Britain.

It is because of these symbolic roles that debate about the monarchy can become so emotionally charged. Arguments about it are often proxies for deeper contests over the nature of the UK, its history and its character. The British people have not, by and large, seen their monarchy as simply another part of the constitutional apparatus of the state: their relationship with it has been considerably more interesting, and often more personal, than that.

In this chapter we shall explore these symbolic roles, and how they relate to modern Britain. We shall discuss the historic evolution of the monarchy, tracing its remarkable ability to adapt to changing times while simultaneously preserving a national myth of continuity and stability. We shall examine public attitudes towards the monarchy – still providing a strength of support which other institutions can only envy. And we shall discuss the character of the society which the monarchy serves. Britain is changing, sociologically and constitutionally. What are the implications of such change for the monarchy? Does the monarchy in its present form meet the needs of modern Britain?

Evolution and symbolism

The British monarchy is one of the longest-established royal houses in the world, claiming 1,000 years of unbroken lineage.

This has given the UK one of its most dominant self-images, that of historical continuity. The British tend to see themselves as an ancient nation which has evolved without revolution over centuries, and the thousand-year unbroken lineage of the monarchy is both proof and symbol of this.

In fact, of course, the lineage of the monarchy is not unbroken. On several occasions tenuous familial connections have been used to fill gaps in direct succession, while monarchical rule was interrupted altogether by the Puritan Commonwealth, following the Civil War, in the mid-seventeenth century. Indeed, the Crown has only been 'British' for 400 years, since the unification of the Scottish and English kingdoms.

The English Crown emerged during the eighth and ninth centuries, as Kings such as Offa and Alfred the Great began to unify the many separate kingdoms that had existed in Britain since the departure of the Romans. Centralised systems of government were developed by the Saxon and Danish kings, a process that continued after the Norman Conquest. Until 1603 the English and Scottish Crowns were separate. Following the death of Elizabeth I without an heir, King James VI of Scotland (I of England) acceded to the English throne, and a single monarch reigned within the British Isles. The formal creation of the UK as a unified state, however, was not completed until the Acts of Union with Scotland in 1707, and with Ireland in 1801.

The development of the monarchy as we know it today, the transition from autocracy to democracy, has been a gradual one. The development of more constitutional government arguably began in 1215 with the Magna Carta, 'an attempt to define anew the king's powers and his duties towards his subjects'.[3] Following the 'Glorious Revolution' and the accession of William and Mary in 1688, monarchs slowly lost their executive powers in the course of the late eighteenth and nineteenth centuries and became increasingly subject to Parliament. By the abdication crisis of 1936 – when the Prime Minister effectively ordered King Edward VIII to relinquish the throne if he would not desist from marrying an American divorcee deemed unsuitable to be Queen – the power of Parliament over the sovereign could no longer be in any doubt. The long history of the monarchy may give the appearance of stability and permanence, but in fact it masks a continual process of evolution in both its constitutional role and its symbolic status within the nation.

Tradition and adaptation

For many people the attraction of monarchy has been as a living link to British history, a cord attaching the nation today to its own past. Running through a thousand years of history, that thread provides a powerful symbol of stability and tradition. For many people it helps define their own British identity. Yet this is something of a paradox, for the representation of stability has been accompanied by a remarkable adaptability. The monarchy has not promoted social change. But it has not resisted it. Indeed, the institution's durability is in part due precisely to its capacity to adapt – albeit sometimes slowly – to the prevailing political, social and cultural trends of the society in which it is embedded. The rise and fall of the British Empire provides a telling example: when Britain became an expanding empire, the monarchy became its highest symbol, with Victoria as Empress of India; when the empire transformed into the Commonwealth of Nations, the monarchy embraced that ideal too and Queen Elizabeth II projected herself as its principal protector and active Head.

In the 20th century in particular the monarchy was alive to the development of democracy and to shifts in popular culture. King George V was an especially important royal 'moderniser' in this respect. Careful not to be too closely affiliated with the drowning empires of Russia and Germany, he actively engaged himself with the emerging ideology of social democracy. Even though the Tsar, Nicolas II, was his first cousin, he refused the imperial family of Russia political asylum in Britain. He encouraged in 1924 the idea that the new Labour Party should have experience of government. It was George V who sensed the impact of sociological and cultural changes, such as the emergence of the nuclear family, and internalised them within the monarchy. He deliberately made use of new media such as radio and newsreels, and was the first monarch to attend a Cup Final.

The monarchy continues to adapt to social and constitutional change. Devolution provides a significant instance. The creation in 1999 of the new Scottish Parliament and the National Assembly of Wales represent very significant constitutional developments, and the Queen has embraced them gracefully. Her speech in 1999 before the Scottish Parliament in Edinburgh, in which she proclaimed the significance and value of devolution, once again ensured that the monarchy was associated with modernity and not with the past.

Ceremony, glamour and public service

In its symbolic functions monarchy seeks resonance in wider society, and for many people it is clear that this is experienced in an almost emotional way. This almost personalised relationship is sustained in part by the mystery and pageantry of its ceremonial occasions, bringing a kind of glamour to public life. But the monarchy has also derived strength from the reciprocity implied by its notion of duty.

Few would deny that the ceremonial role of royalty is one of its central features. Though shared in some part by all heads of state, the ceremony associated with monarchy, and with the British monarchy in particular, tends to be grander and more deeply rooted in historicism and tradition. Monarchy adds, in Churchill's words, 'a splash of colour' to public life. Set-piece events such as coronations and royal funerals, jubilees and marriages, and annual rites such as the State Opening of Parliament, are richly dressed in pageantry. Much of this has in practice evolved along with other aspects of royal life, and many royal 'traditions' are in fact relatively modern inventions, often Victorian in origin. Indeed new ones are being added all the time. The historian Linda Colley notes, for example, that the pageantry around royal weddings is largely a 20th century construction.[4] Owing to the long gap between succeeding monarchs, however, these 'innovations' tend to occur over generations, and thus appear to remain static within the lifetimes of those that observe them.

This is an interaction with society that has successfully been maintained for several hundred years. It was well illustrated in the Queen's Golden Jubilee celebrations in 2002. Here the monarchy sought to attach icons of popular and youth culture to itself through the pop concert held in Buckingham Palace Gardens, and at the same time to reflect the nation's multiculturalism in the composition of the civil carnival that accompanied the more traditional military parade. It was noticeable how the Jubilee of 2002 contrasted with that of 1977. The latter was a much more formal and 'regal' event, reflecting the position of the institution in British society at that time. The change demonstrates how the presentation of monarchy shifts over time. Today celebrity is replacing tradition as the popular face of royalty, a transition influenced powerfully by the late Princess of Wales. This should come as no surprise. In modern times civic society must seek:

'[...]some way of providing civic institutions with a means of infusing themselves with glamour... society needs ceremony, symbols, and stars to sprinkle a little magic dust over its affairs.' [5]

In other countries, such as the USA, this role is well filled by the stars of film, television and music. In Britain, it is royalty which has become the pinnacle of the celebrity culture. Indeed in its public engagements and charitable patronage, and in the constant flow of photographic appearances in tabloid newspapers and magazines, the royal family provides what might be described as a 'public sector' version of what is elsewhere a private enterprise celebrity industry. This new version of royal celebrity is two-edged, however. It adds glamour but it brings intense exposure too. The publicity which surrounded Charles' and Diana's marriage, their separation and divorce created immense pressures for the institution.

The Princess of Wales did not only bring glamour to the image of royalty. She also provided a focus for a new, personalised relationship between the public and the royal family. A great deal has been written about the emotional impact which Diana had on British national life. Some have argued that the public reaction to her death involved 'a shifting of the boundaries of the normal'. An estimated 1.3 million bouquets were laid at symbolically significant sites nationwide, at an estimated cost of some £25m.[6] This was not simply a question of scale. As Anthony Barnett has argued:

'...through their enormous congregations and the oceans of flowers, cards, letters, poems and contributions to condolence books ... millions manifested a desire to be represented differently.' [7]

Yet there have been other occasions when the British public has been intensely moved by a royal death. When George VI died in 1952, for instance, the nation was similarly taken aback by its own sense of shock. 'The King's death really has swamped politics,' wrote Richard Crossman, recording that the office of the *New Statesman* was convulsed by a debate about whether the magazine's front page should carry a black border or not. More dramatic still was the reaction to the premature death of the much admired Prince Consort in 1861. People spoke of that event as a catastrophe, and wondered at a loss that had made 'thoughtful men and maidens, with unrestrained tears, exhibit such emotion'. In adopting behaviour normally associated with personal grief, royal mourners have demonstrated how intensely 'a fantasy relationship with people we do not know'[8] can be felt. There are not many institutions or their incumbents which can provoke such reaction.

This sense of personal relationship owes something to the idea of duty which the modern monarchy expresses towards its subjects and the nation. The commitment to service of the present Queen is a crucial part of the respect and affection in which she is widely held. Many survivors of the bombing of East London during the Second World War similarly felt intense affection for the late Queen Mother because of her continued residence in London during that period, when Buckingham Palace itself was bombed. The images of the royal family walking through debris in London's East End became an immensely powerful symbol of commonality with the threatened subjects of the nation.

The symbolism of duty, even of sacrifice, is an important part of the idea of monarchy; it was fundamental to the development of kingship in earlier societies. It is expressed eloquently in the coronation service, where the monarch dedicates him or herself 'to a life of selfless service and duty'.[9] The burden of kingship has historically been expressed in military duty; this is why members of the royal family still serve in the armed forces. But increasingly, duty has been defined in more conventional forms of public service.

The philanthropic aspects of royalty, such as the patronage and support of voluntary organisations, have been present since the late eighteenth century, when they were revived by George III and Queen Charlotte. However, they have become more prominent and central during the last fifty years. Indeed, the philanthropic work of the monarch and royal family has now become the dominant expression of the longstanding value of duty, as political and constitutional functions have receded. Increasingly, members of the royal family have focused their attention and activities on groups in society needing support and on social, cultural and charitable causes. Through the Prince's Trust, the Prince of Wales has made a particular effort to focus on marginalised groups – notably young people in inner cities, particularly from ethnic minorities. In associating itself with such philanthropic activities, the monarchy has reaffirmed both its importance to national life and its relevance to a changing society. Indeed, to some extent, the popularity of different members of the royal family has come to be measured by their involvement and assiduity in fulfilling public engagements.

Public attitudes to the monarchy

Of all the things that can be said of the British monarchy, perhaps the most certain is that it remains popular, sometimes in spite of the reputations of its individual members. This popularity is something that it shares with other monarchies across Europe, and which marks it out from other public institutions.

Unsurprisingly, there is a wealth of opinion polling data on attitudes towards the monarchy.[10] Much, however, deals with fairly transient issues (whether Charles should marry Camilla, for instance) and few questions are regularly repeated, making it difficult to examine trends in public opinion over time. Nevertheless, some longitudinal data do exist, enabling some broad assertions to be made.

Over the last decade, a fairly consistent 70 per cent of the British public have said that they would rather Britain remained a monarchy than become a republic. However, a significant minority (one in five) describe themselves as broadly republican. Given the number of readings we have for this question, and the turbulent events within the royal family over the period, there has been remarkably little fluctuation in views.

Table 1: If there were a referendum on the issue, would you favour Britain becoming a republic or remaining a monarchy? (Mori)

	1993	1994	1997	1998	1999	2000	2002
	%	%	%	%	%	%	%
Become a republic	18	20	18	16	16	19	19
Remain a monarchy	69	71	73	74	74	70	74
Don't know	14	9	9	10	10	11	7

The level of support is comparable with that found in other European monarchies. In Sweden for example, a country with a deeply embedded left of centre politics, a poll in 2002 found that 66 per cent supported the monarchy, compared to 17 per cent favouring abolition in favour of a republic.[11] In other countries, support was even higher, with more than 90 per cent of Danes [12] and 80 per cent of the Dutch[13] supporting their monarchy.

The headline figures in the UK suggest that there is little enthusiasm for abolishing the monarchy altogether. However, if we consider questions which allow for a third option – some kind of reform of the royal family – support for the institution in its current form falls somewhat. Table 2 shows responses to three different, but very similar, questions asked between 1992 and 2002. Responses show considerable stability over time, but also demonstrate that, once we add reform to the equation, the proportion that would prefer the monarchy to remain as it is drops to around a half. A third would opt for a reformed monarchy of some kind, and around one in ten for a republic. So, among those who opt for a republic when the choice is simply that versus the monarchy (around 20 per cent in Table 1), some would be content with reform rather than abolition.

Table 2: Do you think the monarchy should be left as it is now, radically reformed or abolished altogether? (NOP, 2002). Thinking about the royal family or monarchy in Britain, which of the following do you think should happen? The monarchy should: remain as it is; be reformed; be abolished (NatCen, 1996). In your view should the monarchy remain as it is, be modernised or be abolished? (Gallup, 1992)

	1992	1996	2002
	%	%	%
Remain as it is	51	51	54
Reform or modernisation	31	34	30
Monarchy should be abolished	13	9	12

Despite this apparent stability in views, there has been a notable decline in the belief that the monarchy is of great significance to Britain. In 1984, over three quarters of people thought that Britain would be worse off without the monarchy. By 2002, just under half agreed. Although the proportion thinking Britain would be better off has increased (from 5 to 13 per cent over the same period), this group is outweighed by those who simply think the abolition of the monarchy would make no difference to Britain (up from 16 to 37 per cent). See Table 3.

This interpretation is backed up by other surveys. For instance, the British Social Attitudes survey[14] found that, between 1983 and 1994, the proportion saying that the continuation of the monarchy was 'very important' for Britain halved, from 65 to 32 per cent; for several years after that it remained stable: recently it has slightly increased, although it is too early to know whether this is a long term trend.

Table 3: On balance, do you think Britain would be better off or worse off if the monarchy was abolished, or do you think that it would make no difference? (Mori)

	1984	1987	1989	1992	1994	1996	1998	2000	2002
	%	%	%	%	%	%	%	%	%
Better off	5	5	7	14	14	17	15	10	13
Worse off	77	73	58	50	47	34	53	50	46
No difference	16	20	34	32	35	42	29	37	37
Don't know	2	2	1	4	4	6	3	3	4

These figures suggest three clear messages. First, there is majority support for the monarchy to continue in its current form, though a significant minority would favour some kind of reform. Second, although views have fluctuated from one year to another, attitudes towards the desirability of the monarchy have essentially changed little over the last decade. Finally, despite a sizeable majority supporting the institution, over the last twenty years there has been a marked fall in the belief that the monarchy matters, and that its survival is important for Britain.

Table 4: How important or unimportant do you think it is for Britain to continue to have a monarchy? (NatCen)

	1983	1994	1996	1998	2000	2002
	%	%	%	%	%	%
Very important	65	32	32	28	31	37
Quite important	22	34	35	36	34	33
Not important	11	23	22	24	25	21
Should be abolished	3	10	11	10	10	8

Shades of opinion

Not surprisingly, views about the monarchy vary considerably from one group to another. The most pronounced differences in view relate to age. The 65-plus age group are around twice as likely as those under 34 to think the monarchy is very important for Britain, and are much less likely to support abolition altogether. However, even among the young, half see the continuation of the monarchy as very or quite important for the country. And, while they are the most supportive of a republic, fewer than one in six take this view.

Table 5: Importance for Britain of continuing to have a monarchy ((NatCen, 2002)

	18-24	25-34	35-44	45-54	55-65	65+
	%	%	%	%	%	%
Very important	18	29	37	33	44	50
Quite important	32	35	31	32	33	33
Not important	32	23	22	30	16	10
Should be abolished	15	10	9	5	7	7

This link between age and views about the monarchy has led some to claim that Britain will become less and less supportive of the institution over time, as younger generations gradually replace older ones. There is likely to be some degree of truth in this – younger people are less likely to value the monarchy and their views on this are unlikely to change simply by virtue of their getting older (as opposed to changing in response to particular events). However, most of the change in people's views that we have seen so far has occurred among all age groups – even older people are less supportive now than they once were. In 1983, three quarters of the 65-plus age group thought the continuation of the monarchy to be very important for Britain; now only a half of this age group do so. So future trends will depend as much upon current events which affect views about royalty as they will on one generation replacing another.

Common socio-economic indicators (such as class and education) are not strongly linked to views about the importance of the monarchy, with some research pointing towards stronger republican feeling among the better educated middle classes and others contradicting this.

To some degree, opinion about the monarchy varies according to religious background. Anglicans are in general more supportive than any other groups and are twice as likely as those who are not religious to see the continuation of the monarchy as being very important (52 and 25 per cent respectively). This is not entirely explained by the older age profile of this group; their pro-monarchy views remain even when this is taken into account.

Views also differ by political party support. Conservative identifiers are twice as likely as Labour or Liberal Democrat supporters to think the continuation of the monarchy is very important for Britain (57, 28 and 35 per cent respectively). Support for abolition is highest among Labour identifiers and those who do not support any political party (11 and 12 per cent). Again, these differences remain even once the different age profiles of these groups are taken into account.

Geographically, support for the monarchy is lowest in Scotland, where people are nearly half as likely as those in England to see the continuation of the monarchy as very important, and are twice as likely to support abolition. This is partly (but not wholly) linked to the fact that feelings of 'pride' in being British are lower in Scotland than elsewhere. In fact, British national pride has an exceptionally strong link with views about the monarchy. Nearly a half (47 per cent) of those who say they are very proud to be British think the continuation of the monarchy to be very important (and only six per cent support its abolition). Among those who are not very proud, or not at all proud, only 14 per cent think the monarchy is very important, and one in five would like it to be abolished.

Table 6: Importance for Britain of continuing to have a monarchy (NatCen 2000)

	England	Scotland	Wales
	%	%	%
Very important	32	17	31
Quite important	34	32	37
Not important	24	32	22
Should be abolished	9	18	10

There are, then, notable differences of opinion in relation to age, religion, political party support, national identity, country of residence, and one's 'pride' in being British. The decline in the view that the continuation of the monarchy is important for Britain has taken place among all these groups, rather than being confined to one group or another.

Changing Britain

Much as the monarchy continues to change so too does the country over which it presides. The changing character of Britain has often led the evolution in the form and function of royalty. As has been discussed, the British monarchy has been surprisingly successful in adapting to changed circumstances – certainly more so than some of its now defunct European cousins.

Diversity is not a new feature of British society and the monarchy has always operated differently in different parts of Britain, reflecting national variations. However, Britain is arguably now changing more rapidly than in other periods, constitutionally, socially and culturally. Much of this comes from the acceleration of social development driven by new technologies and by the processes of individualisation and globalisation, which has seen many of the old patterns of family, class and authority realign themselves within generations. The Britain of 2003 is markedly different from the country which saw the Coronation of Elizabeth II, and the fluidity of social relations presents challenges for all institutions, including those traditionally nimbler than the monarchy.

However, there are other more specific structural changes, both social and constitutional, which have particular implications for a hereditary institution which seeks to represent and symbolise a unified idea of Britain. The first is the changing character of the nation state, exemplified by the pressures and processes of devolution. The second is the shifting cultural conception of nationality brought about by multiculturalism.

Devolution

Since 1997, Britain has been subject to far-reaching constitutional reform, most notably through the devolution of political power to its constituent nations. Scotland has seen the reconstitution of its Parliament, and Assemblies have been created in Wales and Northern Ireland. The development of regional government in England, led by the creation of the Greater London Authority, creates other centrifugal forces.

In some ways this reverses the process of unification which created the British composite state under the Crown. However, devolution may also strengthen the role of supranational unifying institutions such as the British monarchy, which have historically acted to promote national cohesion. In fact, the monarchy is potentially better adapted to deal with this than other constitutional institutions in the UK; it might be argued that it is one of the few major civil institutions, along perhaps with the BBC, which is wholly British as opposed to English, Scottish or Welsh.[15]

However, it is clear that the monarchy is perceived differently in the various parts of the UK. There is certainly polling evidence of a growing lack of interest in the institution in Scotland and Wales. This became particularly noticeable during the 2002 Golden Jubilee celebrations. In England the Jubilee was universally seen as a great success. But in neither Scotland nor Wales did it attract anything like the same level of enthusiasm, and in much of Northern Ireland it was not celebrated at all. It is worth noting that the relative lack of interest in Scotland is a recent development: there was much greater interest in 1977 at the time of the Silver Jubilee events.[16]

The heir to the throne is the Prince of Wales. But in Wales itself there is a widespread perception that Prince Charles does not take his title as seriously as he might. His failure in particular to use the Welsh language, to acquire a property in Wales, or even to visit very often, almost certainly has some negative impact on the monarchy's popularity there. Attempts to develop the royal presence in Wales, such as the invented investiture ceremony for Prince Charles, have tended to be seen as unconvincing. It is notable that the national anthem is not universally used in Wales. The Welsh have a national anthem of their own, *Yr Hen Wlad fy Nhadau.*

The situation in Scotland is somewhat different. Indeed the royal family has always been rather adept at appearing Scottish while in Scotland, for example by using the Scottish regalia. The Queen (following the late Queen Mother) has been particularly good at maintaining her Scottish connections, which are certainly much more convincing than the royal presence in Wales. However, this may simply be a product of the personalities of the two Queens, and there is some doubt that Prince Charles will continue this relative visibility in Scotland. Certainly, sending Prince William to a Scottish university has not been generally seen as a great success in strengthening the monarchy's 'Scottishness' – there is some feeling that this has been a half-hearted attempt to manufacture a royal Scottish expert. Indeed, there is a sense in which the English perception of the royal family's Scottishness is not shared by Scots, who feel that the royal family treats Scotland simply as a holiday destination.[17]

There are a number of possible explanations for the difference in attitudes to the monarchy in Scotland and England. There are obvious sociological distinctions between the two countries, and Scotland's political centre of gravity is generally further to the left, which might account for a greater resistance to an unelected institution. But part of the reason is a sense that the institution is essentially English. Scotland after all does not share the myth of 1000 years of an unbroken royal dynasty. The notion of a dual monarchy is increasingly felt. The Queen has a distinct standard in Scotland and in theory the monarch represents Scotland's equal place in the union. Yet the failure to acknowledge the fact that the Scottish title of the Queen should be Elizabeth I sends its own signal. The result is a relationship with the monarchy in Scotland which is substantially different from that which prevails in England. There is limited animosity to the institution, but it is not a fundamental part of Scottish national identity as it might be to an English or British one.

Cultural diversity

Alongside its territorial diversity, Britain is now more socially heterogeneous than in the past. Class identities are weaker and more fractured, families take many forms, and geographic mobility has weakened the ties of traditional community. Perhaps the single most influential factor in the changing face of British society over the last fifty years has been the arrival and integration of significant black and Asian communities, alongside many other ethnicities. Britain is now home to numerous languages and to people of all faiths and none. Identity has become more complex, with layers of allegiance and attachments associated with place, faith and culture. A mono-cultural conception of Britishness is no longer valid. This inevitably challenges the ability of a hereditary Head of State to represent the country to itself.

The monarchy is frequently characterised as a symbol or even embodiment of British nationhood. Yet in its representation of the 'imagined community' of Britain, only a limited version of national identity is available to the monarchy. While any institution faces difficulties in representing multiple identities, a hereditary one faces an additional problem in that its character is more or less fixed. Institutionally and personally, the British monarchy is defined by religion, by class, by territory (England, and particularly Southern England), by race, and by culture.[18]

Yet at the same time the monarchy is perhaps more capable of reflecting positively the identities of black and Asian Britons than it might at first appear. This is because of its association with the Commonwealth. Many of Britain's ethnic minorities retain links to countries of origin which are themselves linked to the Queen through the Commonwealth – and in some cases where she is Head of State. When the Queen visited Jamaica in 2001 it was notable for the very positive response this attracted from many black people of Jamaican descent in England. Nevertheless it is clearly true that the hereditary nature of the monarchy makes more substantial change in the institution's representativeness a difficult and slow process. An elected Head of State with a limited term of office can be drawn from any part of society, reflecting the nation as it is now and allowing for variation even within a generation. Such a variation is likely to take much longer in a hereditary institution.

There is in fact little polling evidence on how the monarchy is perceived in Britain's non-white communities. However, some commentators refer to the experience of the Golden Jubilee and (especially) Diana's funeral, when many black and Asian Britons were seen in the crowds. Indeed there is anecdotal evidence from Hackney in east London at the time of Princess Diana's death, which revealed as much mourning in Afro-Caribbean as in white communities. The writer Anthony Barnett has suggested of Diana's funeral that:

'It was a naturally integrated, multiracial national mourning. I am not saying that every black person identified with Diana ... [but] each section of British society had an equal claim on the experience. It was in effect the first Anglo-British state occasion from which no one felt excluded because of their background.'[19]

It would not necessarily be surprising if younger generations of black and Asian people held attitudes towards the monarchy very similar to those of their white contemporaries. In general, surveys show that the attitudes of first generation immigrants are noticeably distinct, but after the third generation opinions converge with those of the majority community.[20]

Anecdotal evidence suggests that one reason for the support for the monarchy amongst black and Asian Britons is because it is seen as a test of loyalty. The monarchy is the symbol of the state and by professing support for it the immigrant can 'prove' his or her allegiance. It might be assumed that this would only be an issue for a first generation migrant and that for a third generation black person national loyalty would not be in question.

But racism complicates the picture. For some members of ethnic minorities it would appear that the royal family represents much that is old-fashioned and socially exclusive about Britain; but for others it is a non-political institution to which loyalty comes relatively easily. While the difficulties of personal relationships and behaviour which have beset the royal family in recent years appear to have dented the affection of the white population for the monarchy, for some members of ethnic communities these seem to be taken more as general symptoms of the moral decadence of Western society than as specific weaknesses of the institution.[21]

These factors combine to produce a complex pattern of attitudes to the monarchy, reflecting the multifaceted relationship between the monarchy and British society. It is a relationship often based as much on emotional responses as on rational consideration. There is general and robust support in public opinion, but it is not unconditional. For the most part, Britons seem to want their monarchy to continue, but they want it to be more relevant to them and the way they live now. And as Britishness becomes a more diffuse identity, so the importance that the British attach to the institution lessens. Our affection for the monarchy, and our fascination for royalty, remains – but the terms on which they are held are changing.

Notes

1 Cited in *The Nature of the Crown: a legal and political analysis*, Maurice Sunkin and Sebastian Payne, OUP 1999

2 'The golden jubilee: Ben Pimlott tells why we are obsessed by royalty', Ben Pimlott, *The Independent on Sunday*, 2nd June 2002

3 *The Oxford Illustrated History of the British Monarchy*, John Cannon and Ralph Griffiths, OUP 1998, p. 125

4 David McCrone in oral evidence presented to the Commission on 21st November 2002

5 'A queen's ransom' by Evan Davies, *Monarchies: What are Kings and Queens for?*, Tom Bentley and James Wilsdon (eds), Demos 2002

6 Pimlott, *op. cit.*

7   *This Time: The Constitutional Revolution*, Anthony Barnett, Vintage 1997, p.124

8   Pimlott, *op. cit.*

9   *God Save the Queen: The spiritual dimension of the Monarchy*, Ian Bradley, Darton Longman and Todd 2002, p. 93

10 The data used in this section come from a range of sources - Mori, Gallup, NOP as well as the National Centre for Social research. Data are available on their websites

11 Sifo Polling Institute, June 2002

12 'See the queen by request or bump into her at a shop', Stephen Bates, The *Guardian*, 14th April 2001

13 'Going Dutch ensures the future is Orange', Andrew Osborn, The *Guardian*, 14th April 2001

14 Details of the British Social Attitudes survey series can be found in *British Social Attitudes Survey, 19th Report*, A Park, J Curtice, K Thompson, L Jarvis and C Bromley, National Centre for Social Research 2002

15 Linda Colley, in oral evidence presented to the Commission on 21st November 2002

16 David McCrone, in oral evidence presented to the Commission on 21st November 2002

17 *ibid.*

18 Bhikhu Parekh, in oral evidence presented to the Commission on 19th November 2002

19 Barnett *op. cit.*

20 Parekh, *op. cit.*

21 *ibid.*

Chapter 3

Approaches to Monarchy

The pervasiveness of the image of royalty in newspapers and magazines is coupled with a less well remarked centrality of the institution to the British constitution. The combination of constitutional and symbolic roles tends to prompt strong emotional and political responses, both positive and negative. Any agenda for reform must be framed within that context.

Of course the UK is not the only constitutional monarchy. In the European Union alone there are six others. They have much in common, though all have distinctive national features too. And although the executive presidencies of France and the USA form the popular archetype of modern republics, constitutional presidencies – where the Head of State fulfils a limited constitutional role – are equally common.

In thinking about possible reform to the office of Head of State, the experience of other countries could provide valuable lessons. However most debate on this subject in the UK has remained resolutely domestic in character. Often bound up with the personalities of the particular members of the royal family, the debate has been markedly polarised. It is framed on the one hand by a traditionalist defence of monarchy, on the other by convinced republicanism. Between these two poles, there remains a great deal of space for more nuanced argument. In this chapter we examine how both constitutional monarchies and non-executive presidencies work in other countries, and try to unpick the British debate. The chapter concludes with the Commission's own approach to, and principles for, the reform of the monarchy. These principles inform the rest of the report.

Experience in other European countries

Six other countries within the European Union have a hereditary monarch as their Head of State. Most European Union states however are republics, either executive presidencies, such as France, where the President is also the head of government, or constitutional presidencies, such as Ireland, where the President takes a formal, non-political role. By examining examples of such non-executive heads of state – whether elected, appointed or hereditary – we can put the UK's constitutional arrangements in an international context. This is a useful starting point for thinking about possible reform of the British system.

Most of the European monarchies, like the British, have long histories and have derived their legitimacy over time, originally from their supremacy in pre-democratic constitutions. Unlike the British monarchy, however, all of the other European monarchies are subject to constraint by a written constitution.

In two cases the monarchy has been legitimised by a referendum. The Norwegian monarchy was confirmed in a plebiscite held at the time of cession from the Swedish King in 1905. In Spain, the popular legitimacy of the monarchy has come about more recently. Although King Juan Carlos II succeeded General Franco automatically in 1975, ending the anomaly of a kingdom without a king, the monarchy was confirmed by a popular referendum in 1978. It is generally acknowledged that King Juan Carlos II played an important role in his country's transition to democracy, and in unifying Spain during a period of dramatic decentralisation. His strong declaration for democracy during an attempted coup in 1981 particularly endeared him and the institution to the country.

Although not always quite as dramatically, most other monarchs play a similarly important symbolic role in unifying their countries. As the constitutional academic Vernon Bogdanor has put it:

'In Belgium, it is sometimes said that the king is the only Belgian, everyone else being either Fleming or Walloon.' [1]

The role as national figurehead, representing the state, is in part simply a symbolic one – receiving visiting foreign dignitaries, making overseas visits, appearing at public events and ceremonies, and bestowing civil honours. But there are also a number of more formal roles that heads of state typically undertake as a symbol of the nation in the international context. Many have responsibility for accrediting foreign ambassadors and for signing their own country's ambassadors' letters of accreditation to other countries. Some, such as the Swedish, also act as Honorary Chief of certain military companies and as the 'most distinguished representative of the Swedish defence forces'.

Constitutional presidents also have important symbolic roles. The republics of Germany and Italy both emerged from the defeat of the Second World War, although in Italy there was a short-lived constitutional monarchy ended by popular referendum in 1948. In both countries the Presidents explicitly exist to personify their nation's unity and to guarantee the constitution, important considerations in both cases given the circumstances of their inception. In Germany, the President is elected by the Federal Convention, an electoral college derived from the Federal Parliament and the regional parliaments. The President serves a term of five years, and is limited to two consecutive terms. In Italy, the President is elected by the Parliament every seven years.

The selection of all the constitutional monarchs is by hereditary succession. This is always by primogeniture, that is to the eldest child. Some countries, such as Norway, the Netherlands and Belgium, have no gender preference. Others, like the UK, favour sons. There is, of course, no unnatural limit to the term of office. All European monarchs, except the British monarch, swear on accession to uphold the constitution and the law. However, the manner in which Europe's monarchs are crowned varies rather more substantially. In Sweden there is no coronation ceremony at all, while in the Netherlands monarchs are not crowned, but invested as heads of state; although the investiture takes place in a church, the ceremony is entirely secular.

In a number of countries the relationship between monarch and organised religion extends beyond the coronation ceremony. There is a constitutional requirement to profess the state religion in some of the Nordic countries: in Denmark and Norway, although not Sweden, monarchs must be full members of the Evangelical-Lutheran Church. In the Netherlands, Belgium and Spain – and in the republics of Italy and Germany – there is no state religion and no religious constraints on the office of Head of State. This reflects the religious composition and self-image of the countries concerned, underlying the symbolic relationship between monarch and nation.

In addition to their purely representative role, both monarchs and presidents occupy a pivotal position in the constitution of their countries. These constitutional duties are broadly similar across both the monarchies and non-executive presidencies, although the extent of discretionary power at their disposal to fulfil those duties varies considerably. In general terms, heads of state act as constitutional guarantors, bestowing legitimacy upon the appointment of senior public offices, the formation of governments, the status of parliaments and the enacting of legislation.

Perhaps unsurprisingly, constitutional presidents tend to hold greater discretionary powers in these areas, although these powers vary. The Italian President, for example, has the power to dissolve and summon both houses of Parliament, but only after consulting their Speakers, rather than the Executive. In Germany the President is not even symbolically responsible for the appointment of the Federal Chancellor. Rather, his role is merely to propose formally a candidate for election, and then to formalise the appointment of the elected candidate. However, the President does have discretionary power over the assent to legislation, and this has been used on a small number of occasions. Most recently, for example, President Von Weizsaecker, in office until 1999, declined to sign a law to amend an Air Traffic Act because it contravened an article of the constitution.

The Danish constitution resembles the British in that all governmental powers are formally vested in the monarch. Formally, the monarch holds executive and legislative power and is the highest authority in all matters. In practice, Queen Margrethe II exercises these powers on advice, although she retains the right to dissolve parliament and call a general election. She also enacts legislation and appoints the Prime Minister and all other ministers of the government, on the advice of the leaders of the political parties. They inform her of their allegiances and she appoints the one with the greatest support.

The Dutch Queen plays a similarly significant role in the formation of new governments. After a parliamentary election, acting on the recommendation of political leaders and the Speakers of the houses of parliament, the Queen appoints a senior political figure to determine which of the parties are prepared to work together in a coalition government (no party has ever achieved a parliamentary majority in the Netherlands). The Queen then appoints a new government. After their first meeting, the new ministers are sworn in by the Queen and they are appointed by royal decree. The decree is signed by the Queen and co-signed by the Prime Minister on behalf of the other ministers.

According to the constitution, the King of the Belgians reigns but does not govern. Federal legislative power is exerted collectively by the King, the House of Representatives, and the Senate. Within this system, King Albert II retains the power to promulgate and sanction laws, and to establish the regulations and decrees required for the execution of laws. But he does not have the power either to suspend the laws themselves or to dispense from their execution. He also has the formal right to nominate the government and to dissolve parliament.

In Spain, Juan Carlos's constitutional role is far smaller than that of the British monarch, and the constitution has been described as almost republican.[2] Having played an active role in the democratisation of Spain, King Juan Carlos has rarely interfered with the running of the country since restoration. He has devolved ever more power away from the monarchy and now occupies a strictly symbolic role.

Arguably the least politically powerful of Europe's monarchs is Carl XVI Gustaf of Sweden. The Swedish constitution was amended in 1975, two years after his accession, and transferred all remaining royal prerogative powers to the Speaker of the House of Parliament. The Swedish monarch does not dissolve or summon parliament or appoint the Prime Minister, although he does chair the special council meeting to negotiate the basis of a new government after an election.

Plainly, the UK is not unique amongst the European democracies, either in having a constitutional monarch as Head of State, or in the scope of the role that the Head of State, elected or otherwise, performs. Indeed, the British monarch does not enjoy as much discretionary power as some other European heads of state. Some other European monarchies, notably in Sweden and Spain, have far fewer discretionary powers, yet continue to play an important part in public life, commanding considerable popular legitimacy. There is then scope within international experience for a successful constitutional monarchy to be maintained, yet on a different basis from that of the UK.

Debates in the UK

Britain's monarchy is within the range of experience of other European constitutional monarchies. It also shares another feature with them: there is a powerful political debate about its future. In the UK such debate has only become respectable in relatively recent years, and it still occupies a rather marginal area of the wider debate about the British constitution. Yet it undoubtedly exercises considerable passion and no little thought.

The financial cost or benefit of the monarchy is sometimes deployed by those seeking either to abolish or defend the institution. Yet the economic case for or against the monarchy is not particularly powerful. Depending on how it is calculated, the cost of the institution is somewhere between £35 and £60 million a year. This equates to a maximum annual cost per citizen of a little over £1 each or around 2p per week, which is not an excessive amount, and compares favourably with other heads of state.[3] On the other side of the balance sheet, the economic value of the monarchy is difficult to quantify, but is probably fairly marginal. This is especially true for tourism,[4] but also in respect of the purely economic value generated for charities, which, in the absence of the royal family, would presumably be generated by other celebrities. On balance the role of the monarchy in public and charitable works is an important contribution to British society, but the economic benefit or cost of the monarchy is not a useful way of assessing its value. If it is worth having then it is worth it for non-economic reasons – and similarly if it isn't.

The boundaries of the more important debate can be characterised as outright republicanism and traditional monarchism. Between these poles, the complete rejection of the hereditary principle within the constitution and the complete rejection of the need for reform, a nuanced debate can be found.

The arguments against reform, and for the maintenance of what might be described as the 'monarchy of tradition', centre on three core ideas. First, it holds that the system, with the monarch at its apex, works. This is not simply to say that it is preferable to the likely alternatives, although reference is frequently made to the relative popularity of the Queen and relative unpopularity of elected politicians. Proponents of this view do not accept that constitutional monarchy is simply the least bad system on offer. Rather, they argue that the essential strength of a hereditary Head of State is that it ensures constitutional legitimacy by putting the office beyond party politics. By vesting constitutional authority in the Crown, in the person of the monarch, rather than a written document or an elected politician, the constitution retains both flexibility and universalism, ensuring its continued legitimacy. The durability of the British constitutional settlement, and the relatively few crises it has seen, are evidence enough, advocates contend, that that the system does not need fixing.

The second proposition is that the monarchy is a source of stability in a fluid society. It is precisely because so many cultural and social landmarks are shifting that the monarchy needs to be preserved as a 'fixed point' in a rapidly changing world. As deference wanes and social order weakens – and for many but not all proponents of this position, these are seen as changes for the worse – the monarchy represents a set of traditional values around which the country can cohere. In particular, by providing a bridge to the past, the institution underpins a sense of national identity built on history and unity.

Proponents of this view argue that the role of national unifier has been historically important in a state comprising at least four distinct territorial nationalities. As Britain has become more diverse, culturally and socially, over the past half century, so has the importance of this role. This 'social glue' is an important positive role for the monarchy, which belongs to no vested interests and consequently belongs to all. As Vernon Bogdanor argues:

'Provided that a sovereign carries out the constitutional functions in an impartial way, he or she is in a better position to represent the nation as a whole and to be a representative whom everyone can accept.' [5] Further, it is argued that a hereditary Head of State need not maintain rigid class divisions or inhibit modernity; the egalitarian Scandinavians and progressive Netherlands can be cited as illustrations. [6]

Many proponents of this argument are resolutely conservative in other ways. Others, such as Vernon Bogdanor, have noted that the conservatism of the monarchy has in fact assisted in other progressive developments. Both the historical transition from Empire and the constitutional reform agenda of the Blair Governments have been facilitated by the reassuring presence of an 'unchanging' monarchy. Devolution to Scotland and other parts of the UK, without the fragmentation of the state, has been possible because of the cohesive role of a monarch who is neither Scottish nor English, but simply British. By retaining a conservative core to the constitution, it is argued, other radical shifts are made more acceptable to an essentially conservative people.

Finally, reform is rejected by some because the very process would undermine and damage the integrity of the institution. Since the monarchy's most important symbolic function is to provide stability in a rapidly changing world, a structured process of reform would rob the institution of its mystique. The authority of the Crown and monarch in many ways derives from not being questioned or challenged; externally imposed reform would end this, turning a unique, organic authority into simply another state agency. As the Victorian constitutional writer Walter Bagehot famously observed:

'Above all things our royalty is to be reverenced, and if you begin to poke about it you cannot reverence it. When there is a select committee on the Queen, the charm of royalty will be gone. We must not let daylight in upon the magic.' [7]

In any case, it is argued, there is no need for 'reform', as the monarchy naturally adapts and evolves to suit changing times; indeed this is the secret of the monarchy's longevity. Those aspects of the institution that become unacceptable to contemporary society will organically wither, without the need for politicians and others to interfere.

Within these arguments there is often an acceptance of the authority of the monarchy simply because it is the monarchy, a deference which those on the republican side of the argument find unacceptable. For those opposed to Britain's monarchical system, the argument centres on two propositions: first, that the principle of heredity is incompatible with democratic norms; and second, that the character of monarchy – and particularly the British monarchy – acts as a regressive force within society, inhibiting equality and modernity.

For republicans, the central issue is the principle of heredity, which is for them simply unacceptable in a democracy. Not only is selection by birth incompatible with democratic principles of accountability and political choice, it is a fundamental right of citizenship to be able to choose one's representatives, and the denial of that right is seen as insulting. A hereditary Head of State confirms citizens as subjects, servants of the constitution rather than its master.

Moreover, republicans argue, the monarchy is above the law. This is more than simply a question of immunity from prosecution: the monarch is actually outside the law. Currently, no law applies to the monarch unless he or she is specifically mentioned in it. Prosecutions are taken out in the Queen's name and every judge swears allegiance to her.

This constitutional position has symbolic importance, far beyond the legal implications, which permeates the whole of British society. The monarchy, it is argued, helps to perpetuate a rigid class system and an elitist attitude to governance amongst the establishment. The social cohesion that the monarchy provides is an unhelpful one, based on deference rather than equality. As the writer Anthony Holden puts it:

'The monarchy is the glue cementing everything that is rotten about our class-ridden, quango-infested, deeply undemocratic society... It

encourages a culture of privilege and connections rather than merit or achievement.' [8] Furthermore, the monarchy represents a very partial view of British history and society, helping to perpetuate a mythical and outdated version of British national identity. As the Scottish republican writer Tom Nairn has suggested, the monarchy is steeped in the 'glamour of backwardness'.[9] In part this is due to the monarchy's associations with the history of kings and queens and empire, in part the very historicism of a hereditary institution. The product, according to republicans, is a culture of nostalgia, which collides with modernity and prevents Britain from fully engaging with the major issues it faces in the modern world. As the political scientist Stephen Haseler has put it:

'As a symbol of its particular brand of Englishness, as a focus for dwelling on past glories, indeed living in the past, the monarchy knows no peer.' [10]

Entangled with the republican case, though not identical with it, is the argument for a written constitution. Certainly other European monarchies demonstrate that there is no reason why the two cannot co-exist. Anthony Barnett has argued that while the other European countries can be accurately described as constitutional monarchies, the UK is in fact a monarchical constitution.[11] The constitution consists partly of the law and partly of informal, fluid, contemporary habits or actions of the incumbent monarch. Indeed, with a written constitution which described and defined the distribution of powers within the system of government and law, the question of who fills the office of Head of State might become far less significant. An elected Head of State might be preferable, Barnett argues, but it is not the key issue.

As Barnett's position shows, even among those who in principle would prefer an elected Head of State, there are some willing to accept reform rather than abolition. The same is perhaps even more true among those who support the monarchy, with many recognising the need for reform to varying degrees. The debate within these two poles of convinced republicanism and traditionalist monarchism stratifies along the scope and extent of the reform needed, and its motivation – whether the aim is to secure or fundamentally to alter the monarchy. In simple terms the divide is between those who regard the constitutional position of an unelected Head of State as unproblematic, but who want to see some degree of reform to the administration and presentation of the institution; and those who argue that there are also fundamental constitutional concerns with the formal powers of the monarch as currently defined.

For advocates of the former position, acceptable reform tends to be limited to the rules of succession, ending the bar on eldest daughters and Catholics, and to the management of the Royal Household (the civil service of the monarchy). Some accept the need for some 'slimming down' of the royal family; others the rationalisation of their taxation and property holding. For proponents of more radical constitutional reform, however, none of this would be sufficient. For them the focus is on the residual political powers of the monarchy and its wider constitutional primacy. The aim of reform is to give the UK a new constitutional settlement, with a clearly defined role for a non-political, and non-religious, Head of State.

The Commission's approach

The hereditary principle is not one which it is easy to defend in an abstract sense. It would be unusual in the extreme to apply it to any new institution or to use it to replace existing means of selecting for public office – a hereditary judiciary, for example, would be inconceivable. Further, where it exists in existing institutions, such as the House of Lords, there is a general consensus that heredity is not a good basis for positions of power and decision. Ours, rightly, is an age of democracy and meritocracy. Yet the issue facing Britain is not an abstract one. While at a theoretical level we might not wish to start from here, Britain's history and constitutional development have brought us to where we are and cannot simply be wished away. Getting rid of the hereditary monarchy, with all the implications that this would have, is a very different proposition from that of simply not creating one in the design of a constitution from scratch.

The UK's monarchy has several valuable characteristics. The very longevity of the institution provides a valuable rootedness in history, and it has served as powerful unifier or 'social glue' in a country long characterised by diversity and multiple identities. By providing a bridge to the past, the monarchy offers a reassurance of solidity in very fluid times. Similarly, the long period of office and the certainty of succession, neither of which would be possible in an elected system, provide a valuable continuity. Distinct from any electoral system, the hereditary Head of State is not dependent upon political processes, placing the office clearly above sectional interests; certainly, monarchs are not 'owned' by those who put them there.

Another key factor which cannot be ignored by any serious examination of the future of the monarchy is its popularity. Along with the BBC, the monarchy is one of very few truly national institutions, enjoying high levels of support across all parts of British society. As discussed in Chapter 2, public opinion remains consistently behind the monarchy, despite any current difficulties for the incumbents. This popular acceptance of the institution, whilst not sufficient in itself, reinforces our view that the primary issue to be addressed is how the office of Head of State should be reformed, not who occupies it.

However, we do believe that reform is necessary if the monarchy is to survive in its present position within the constitution. Its strengths will not necessarily remain so in a changing society. Unless it represents a shared understanding and common values, an emphasis on history can exclude rather than unify. Continuity can become rigidity. Sectional interests can easily form around a privileged family. And, of course, the popularity of the institution cannot be maintained forever if the individuals within it lose the public's respect. Unless the institution can become more relevant symbolically and more appropriate constitutionally, we believe that the strengths of the current system will increasingly be undermined by the obviously incongruous character of a hereditary apex to an otherwise democratic, pluralist state.

Principles for reform

Our central argument is that the monarchy needs to become better suited to the norms of contemporary Britain, and its role within the system of government and law need to be better defined. In particular the office of Head of State needs to become a properly integrated part of the State rather than being the preserve of a private family. In moving towards this we believe there are five key principles which should guide any reform agenda for Britain's Head of State and the wider institution of the monarchy. These are depoliticisation, separation of the public and private, representativeness, transparency and professionalism.

Depoliticisation

By this we mean removing the residual space for political discretion that still remains within the powers of the Head of State. While such powers have been used rarely in recent times, they remain real powers and are inappropriate for a system where the Head of State is neither elected nor accountable. The presumption should therefore be that the functions and relationships of the Head of State, like other parts of the State, should be clearly defined in law and they should allow no scope for political discretion.

Separation of the public and private

The historical inseparability of the monarchy as an institution from the individual and family who occupy it, has left blurred lines between the public and private elements of the modern institution. This is no longer acceptable in a modern constitution. There now needs to be a clear demarcation between the public office of Head of State and the personal life and family affairs of its incumbent. In entirely private affairs, such as taxation of private income and in relation to the law, the Head of State, the heir and members of the wider royal family should as far as possible be on an equal footing with other citizens.

Representativeness

UK society is increasingly diverse and aspires to greater civil and social equality. In order to fulfil its role as a national unifier the office of Head of State needs to represent Britain as it is and, importantly, as it wishes to be. Clearly the office holder – as with any individual – cannot achieve representativeness in their personal characteristics, and it would be unfair and futile to attempt this. However, representativeness can be achieved in the way that the office and incumbents undertake their duties and relate to the society they serve. In every area of the institution's activities and behaviour the office of Head of State should be characterised by inclusivity; it should actively avoid instances of exclusivity and discrimination and should be seen to associate with all parts of Britain and British society.

Transparency

In financial, administrative, constitutional and legal matters, the opacity that currently surrounds the Head of State is not acceptable in a modern democracy. While mystique can be a legitimate – even valuable – part of the ceremonial functions of the monarchy, it can only undermine the operation of a state institution. There needs to be full disclosure about the public business of the office of Head of State, its finance and administration, and these should be subject to proper public scrutiny and accountability.

Professionalism

The public offices of the Head of State should function as professionally as we would expect from any other important public institution. Amateurism and the blurring of personal and professional roles are not acceptable in the office of Head of State any more than they are in the judiciary, Parliament or civil service. The highest standards of professionalism should be ensured in keeping with the accepted norms of public office.

An agenda for reform framed within these principles offers, we believe, the prospect of realigning the British constitution to match the Britain of today. As such it would represent the constructive evolution of the monarchy to meet changing times, in the best British traditions of consensual reform. The following chapters explain what these principles would mean in practice.

Notes

1   'The *Guardian* has got it wrong', Vernon Bogdanor, The *Guardian*, 6th December 2000

2   'Republican monarchy' by Shaun Riordan, *Monarchies: What are Queens and Kings for?*, Tom Bentley and James Wilsdon (eds), Demos 2002

3   'A queen's ransom' by Evan Davies, *Monarchies: What are Queens and Kings for?*, Tom Bentley and James Wilsdon (eds), Demos 2002

4   Evan Davis, in oral evidence presented to the Commission on 18th November 2002

5   *The Monarchy and the Constitution*, Vernon Bogdanor, OUP 1997

6   Vernon Bogdanor in oral evidence presented to the Commission on 5th September 2002

7   *The English Constitution (2nd ed)*, Walter Bagehot, 1873

8   'From flag-waver to republican', Anthony Holden, The *Guardian*, 1st June 2002

9   *The Enchanted Glass: Britain and Its Monarchy*, Tom Nairn, Vintage 1994

10 'Force of Conservatism' by Stephen Haseler in *Monarchies: What are Kings and Queens for?*, Tom Bentley and James Wilsdon (eds), Demos, 2002

11 Anthony Barnett in written evidence to the Commission

Chapter 4

The Constitutional Position of the Head of State

The pageantry and glamour of the British monarchy surrounds what is, in essence, a functional element of our system of government. In all democracies, there are specific constitutional functions that need to be fulfilled over and above the business of government. In some states, such as the USA and France, these functions are combined with the position of head of government; in others, such as the UK, the Head of State is a separate office, outside the business of politics.

Democratic politics is volatile and contested. Governments are elected to fulfil policy programmes, rarely with anything near universal popular support. They operate within the rules of the constitution and must therefore be subordinate to them. In most systems the principal role of Head of State is to guarantee that the constitution is upheld.

In the UK, famously without a written constitution, the Head of State is also the ultimate source of authority. The powers of executive government, exercised by the Prime Minister, flow from the Royal Prerogative rather than from Parliament. And in relation to the law, the monarch as Head of State occupies a unique position in Britain. In some ways her position is similar to that of other heads of state, elected or hereditary, who enjoy immunities during their term of office. However, formally and symbolically the Queen in the UK is regarded as the fount of law, with public prosecutions undertaken in her name.

In all these areas, there is scope for reform to make the office of Head of State more appropriate to the needs of modern Britain, while maintaining it as a monarchy. The task is to define more clearly the nature and extent of the role, removing residual political discretion, and thereby creating a proper, transparent office of Head of State, regardless of how that office is filled.

This last point – how the office holder is selected – prompts other questions about the constitutional aspects to the Head of State's position. The hereditary principle, naturally, does not allow discretion in who succeeds to the office; the lineage is necessarily prescribed. Yet there is scope for making the rules of succession more consistent with prevailing social attitudes, especially concerning gender and religious discrimination. In this way the office of Head of State can be made more representative of the country it serves.

Succession

The basic principles of hereditary succession are simple, with office passing on death to the next in the bloodline. Yet each system has its own peculiar rules, and the British monarchy is no exception. These rules are in fact the most clearly defined element in the constitutional position of the Head of State, placing constraints of gender and faith on who may succeed. For the most part the rules of succession are set out in the English Act of Settlement of 1701 and other related Acts.

A British monarch is formally recognised immediately on the death of his or her predecessor; there is no interval or interregnum and the duration of Parliament is not affected. The aim is to achieve a seamless transition, reflected in the proclamation: 'the King is dead; long live the King!' The new monarch is sworn in at an Accession Council, to which members of the Privy Council and others are summoned, and it is this body which formally confirms the transition of office to the heir.

The line of succession is determined by primogeniture, specifically an agnatic (male) order of succession. This means that the sons of the monarch and their descendants have precedence over daughters in succeeding to the throne, but daughters take precedence over the monarch's brothers and their descendants who form the next in line. A daughter who succeeds to the throne becomes Queen Regnant and acquires the Crown's powers as though she were king. While the wife or consort of a king takes her husband's rank and style, the constitution has never given any special rank or privileges to the husband of a Queen Regnant, although in practice he may be granted honours by the Crown. The rules of succession embody therefore a systematic male precedence. Although female succession has been a possibility for much longer within Britain than some other European monarchies, this represents a degree of discrimination which in any other walk of life would no longer be acceptable in modern Britain.

There are in addition specific religious constraints placed on who may succeed. The Act of Settlement stipulates that only Protestant descendants of Princess Sophia are eligible to succeed to the throne. In addition, any heir who marries a Catholic is excluded from the succession. These were measures originally designed to disbar Catholics from acceding to the throne at a time of considerable religious tension. However, the rules of succession also disbar non-Christian heirs. In addition, as Supreme Governor of the Church of England, the monarch is required to swear to defend the Anglican Church.

An additional provision is made in the Royal Marriages Act 1772 which forbids members of the royal family from marrying without the consent of the monarch. It requires all members of the royal family in line of succession to ask the monarch's permission to marry. However, the Act also stipulates that if the descendent is over twenty-five years of age and has failed to gain the monarch's consent, notice of the intention to marry can be given to the Privy Council and, unless the marriage is contested by Parliament within twelve months of the notice being given, the marriage can be contracted without the monarch's consent.

The current rules of succession raise a fundamental question for a modern democracy. In the context of increasing cultural diversity, and an expectation of civil and social equality, can institutionalised gender and religious discrimination any longer be acceptable? We believe that it cannot, for symbolic as well as practical reasons, and reform is long overdue. While the question of gender discrimination might not be a practical issue for the foreseeable future – a changed law will affect neither Charles nor William – the current settlement has enormous symbolic implications for gender politics and human rights. In future, therefore, we believe the line of succession should pass to the eldest child, regardless of gender. Now is in fact an excellent time to reform this aspect of the succession, precisely because the next three heirs in line to the throne are male, and reform will therefore not change anyone's existing priority.

Similarly, although the foreseeable line of succession is Protestant, we believe the institutionalised religious discrimination of the current rules of succession should also be abolished. In particular the so-called Catholic bar in the Act of Settlement should be repealed, along with the requirement for the monarch to defend the Anglican faith. The Royal Marriages Act should be repealed at the same time.

In themselves these reforms should be uncontentious; they accord with widely accepted norms of religious freedom and the human rights of individuals to practise their own faith. However, abolishing the religious discrimination within the rules of succession has wider implications, concerned with the monarch's role as Supreme Governor of the Church of England. Clearly such reform opens the theoretical prospect of a non-Anglican taking on the leading role within the Church. Our view is that, rather than this being seen as a barrier to reform, it should raise questions about the nature of the relationship between the Head of State and the Church. We shall address this in more detail in the next chapter.

A more challenging problem here may be the position of the fifteen other independent Commonwealth states for whom the British monarch is also Head of State. Changes to the succession will necessarily have a direct impact on the constitutional affairs of those countries, although the extreme possibility – different countries adopting different rules of succession, and therefore having different members of the British royal family as Head of State – seems highly improbable. There is no question, however, that those countries would need to be consulted about any decision in this field. This question is discussed in greater detail in Chapter 6.

Abdication and retirement

Currently, a monarch's reign can only be ended by death or abdication. The Accession Oath commits a new monarch to serve until death; as a religious oath this inevitably becomes a deeply felt duty. Abdication is sought only in a crisis and as a consequence significant stigma attaches to it.

However, in an era of increasing longevity, the expectation that the Head of State will serve until death may no longer be desirable or even sustainable. We believe therefore that there is a strong case for provision to be made for the voluntary retirement of the monarch. This should include a change in the Accession Oath to recognise that in appropriate circumstances this is an acceptable way to end a reign.

Such a reform would enable a monarch to avoid the problem of being too frail or ill to carry out his or her duties. In addition, such a reform would make the transition from sovereign to heir smoother; if it was known that a monarch planned to retire at a particular time, the heir to the throne could gradually take on more of the monarch's work.

The Netherlands offers a precedent for such an arrangement. In 1948 Queen Wilhelmina abdicated at the age of 58 in favour of Juliana. In turn, in 1980 Queen Juliana, then aged 71, abdicated in favour of her daughter Beatrix. Queen Juliana expressed the hope that she could continue to serve the country after her abdication and indeed went on to become Honorary Chair of the National Committee of the International Year of the Handicapped in 1981. She continued to fulfil public duties until the early 1990s since when she has gradually withdrawn from public life. Another precedent can be found in the Swedish constitution, which provides for parliament to require the retirement of the monarch if he or she has been continuously prevented for a period of six months from carrying out his or her duties or has failed to carry them out.

Some have suggested that abdication in any form undermines the concept of monarchy. Vernon Bogdanor, Professor of Government at the University of Oxford, argues that:

'Hereditary Monarchy has as its consequence that the destiny of the future Sovereign is inescapable. Thus abdication, the voluntary renun-

ciation of Sovereignty, strikes at the very heart of the institution whose central tenet must be that normally succession to the throne is not a matter of choice but automatic. Thus, as soon as the question is raised of who might be best fitted to occupy the throne, the hereditary system comes under challenge. Similarly, as soon as a Sovereign treats the office as one which he or she may voluntarily renounce, the automatic rule of succession comes to be under threat.' [1]

But we do not find this argument compelling, particularly in the light of the Dutch experience and the Swedish constitutional provisions. While a more flexible approach to retirement might diminish some of the mystery surrounding the monarchy, it would not undermine the position of a modern Head of State. On the contrary, the possibility of optional voluntary retirement seems entirely sensible. This should not be taken as a suggestion that the present Queen should retire; our concern is to address constitutional principle and future eventualities, not present individuals.

Constitutional powers and functions

As Head of State, and acting on advice from her Government, the British monarch retains a number of important constitutional powers and duties:

Powers and duties concerned with Parliament

- Summoning, proroguing (that is, discontinuing until the next session without dissolving) and dissolving Parliament
- Opening the new session of Parliament each year and giving a speech from the throne outlining her Government's programme
- Giving Royal Assent to any Bill which has passed all its stages in both Houses of Parliament (or under the terms of the Parliament Acts 1911-49) before it becomes law
- Appointment of the Prime Minister after a general election

Executive powers and duties

- Appointing and dismissing government ministers
- Presiding over meetings of the Privy Council. At these, among other things, Orders in Council made under the royal prerogative or under statute are approved
- To declare war
- To conclude international treaties
- To recognise foreign state and governments
- To annex and cede territory

Other powers and duties

- Conferring peerages and other honours
- Making appointments to many of the most important state offices, including judges, members of the diplomatic corps and colonial officials
- Appointing bishops of the Church of England
- Appointing officers as Commander-in-Chief of the armed services
- Accrediting foreign diplomatic representatives in London
- Representing the United Kingdom on state visits overseas and receiving other nations' heads of states visiting the UK
- Pardoning or showing mercy in exceptional circumstances to those convicted of crimes

Many of these functions – notably those in the second group of executive powers – are actually exercised by the Prime Minister or other ministers in the name of the monarch; they are not properly discretionary powers at all. In the first group, however, concerned with the workings of Parliament, the Head of State retains political discretion over how the powers are exercised. By longstanding convention the monarch does not in fact exercise this discretion, and it would clearly provoke a constitutional crisis if a monarch today were seen to be acting in a politically partial way. But in terms of the constitution it is only convention, not law, which prevents this happening.

We do not believe that it is in anyone's interest for the monarchy to be able, even in theory, to exercise decisions of a highly political nature. It is clearly not acceptable in the modern era for political power to be exercised by an hereditary and unaccountable official. From the monarchy's point of view, any exercise of political discretion in the conduct of the sovereign's duties would precipitate intense criticism and almost certainly a threat to the institution's continued existence, so there is little to be gained by the continued retention of the powers.

We therefore see no real argument for retaining the residual discretion available to the Head of State. Either this discretion is purely theoretical and would never be used, or its use would provoke a constitutional crisis by offending democratic principle. In this section, a number of reforms are presented which could finally depoliticise the office of Head of State, thereby ensuring a proper constitutional role in a modern democracy.

The Royal Prerogative powers

Broadly speaking, the Royal Prerogative powers are the residual non-statutory powers left in the hands of the Crown. The prerogative rights and duties of the Crown, in many cases ill-defined, are remnants of those immunities and powers possessed by medieval kings, both as chief feudal lords and as heads of state. In practice most of the Royal Prerogative powers nominally in the hands of the Head of State are actually exercised as unconstrained powers of the Prime Minister and executive.

These include the powers to conclude treaties, annex and cede territory, recognise foreign states and governments, and – most controversially – to declare war and make peace. The use of the Royal Prerogative effectively means that, in crucial areas, the government does not need to have Parliament's authority to engage in these activities. At the same time the Royal Preogative powers give the Prime Minister huge powers of patronage through the appointments he or she can make to state offices, nominally in the name of the Crown.

We believe that these arrangements are now unacceptable, for two reasons. First, they give unfettered powers to the executive in crucial areas such as the declaration of war which in most countries would require parliamentary assent. Second, it misleadingly associates the exercise of these powers with the Head of State. Our view is that the powers now exercised by the executive should be formally and linguistically separated from the office of Head of State and put on a statutory basis. The term 'Royal Prerogative powers' should be replaced by the terms 'parliamentary' and 'executive' powers which reflects the reality of their use.

Precisely how the various Royal Prerogative powers in this category should be exercised should be a matter for Parliament to decide. As a Commission concerned only with the monarchy, the details are beyond the remit of this report. But on critical matters such as the declaration of war, democratic principle would suggest that power should be exercised by the executive only with Parliament's assent. In areas such as the appointment to state offices, the powers may well be better exercised by bodies independent of both Parliament and executive such as a Judicial Appointments Commission. Parliament may well decide that some powers should remain with the Prime Minister and executive; however, it would formally base these executive powers in Acts of Parliament and in this way end their association with the office of Head of State.

Dissolution and summoning of Parliament

In law, Parliament is the creature of the monarch. Parliament exists because the Head of State summons it, and she similarly dismisses it. In practice, of course, these acts are carried out on the advice of the Prime Minister, but the power is not purely symbolic. From the moment of dissolution, Parliament ceases to exist. This means that for about five weeks, until an election is held and Parliament recalled, there is no official check on the government. More remarkably, the monarch is not legally required to summon a new Parliament immediately; the only law setting down rules for the meeting of Parliament is the Triennial Act of 1694, requiring Parliament to meet once every three years. (In practice Parliament could probably not remain 'un-summoned' for long: income tax requires annual parliamentary authorisation.)

Some have argued for keeping the sovereign's discretionary powers in this area for unpredictable constitutional eventualities. Constitutional expert Rodney Brazier argues that:

'If the government refused to bow to the wishes of the electorate, the Queen's power to dismiss the government... would be the only weapon left to dislodge it.' [2]

However, we do not believe that it is acceptable in a democracy that the dissolution and summoning of Parliament should remain a discretionary power of the Head of State, governed only by convention. Nor is it inevitable in a constitutional monarchy: for example, in Sweden the monarch has no role in the dissolution or summoning of Parliament at all. Our view is that it would be preferable for the dissolution of Parliament to be regulated by statute. The Head of State should therefore only be able to dissolve Parliament in two circumstances: either at its five year term limit, as currently, or on a majority vote in the House of Commons. In addition, we would argue for an amendment to the Representation of the People Act, specifying a maximum interval of six weeks between the dissolution of Parliament and its summoning.

Appointment of the Prime Minister

The Head of State also has responsibility for appointing the Prime Minister. The appointment is again governed by convention giving the incumbent Prime Minister the first opportunity to form a government rather than the leader of the largest political party in the new Parliament. In most circumstances the matter is straightforward, as the UK's electoral system typically produces clear parliamentary majorities for one party. In such circumstances, the leader of the largest party is invited to take office, with a losing incumbent making way.

However, clear majorities do not always occur, and a minority government was formed as recently as 1974. In these circumstances, or in times of national crisis necessitating a 'grand coalition' or National Government, the Head of State has genuine discretion.[3] There are clearly arguments for having a neu-

tral mediator in the parliamentary process of forming a government where the decision is not clear cut. However, there have
been various occasions where the personal political judgement
of the monarch has been involved to a degree that gives cause
for genuine democratic concern. One such occasion was George
V's appointment of Ramsay MacDonald as Prime Minister in the
National Government of 1931, even though he could not command a majority in his own party. The discretionary power in
this case is very real.

This is defended by some as an essential contingency power.
But there are other constitutional monarchies where the Head of
State has little or no role in these circumstances. In Sweden the
monarch does not appoint the Prime Minister at all, while the
Dutch monarch, acting on the recommendation of political leaders and the Speakers of the Houses of Parliament, simply
appoints a senior political figure to determine which of the parties are prepared to work together in a coalition government. It
is not the monarch's place to play this role him or herself.

Consistent with our principle of depoliticising the office of
Head of State, we believe that the discretionary powers in
appointing the Prime Minister should be removed from the
monarch. Specifically, the role of Head of State should simply be
to recognise as Prime Minister whoever can command a majority in the House of Commons. The election of Prime Minister
should be the first item for a new Parliament or in circumstances
where no Prime Minister is in office, and the Speaker should
manage the voting process. This would require codification in
statute of the process by which Prime Ministers are appointed
and governments formed. (This would incidentally have the
additional benefit of formalising the position of the Prime
Minister, which at present is not a statutory position at all.)

Royal Assent to legislation

Acts of Parliament do not become law until they receive Royal
Assent from the Head of State. This is a discretionary power –
the monarch is obliged only by convention, not law, to sign
those Acts which have been through the proper procedures of
Parliament. In practice the monarch's power of Royal Assent has

widely been regarded as a 'non issue' because it has not caused controversy since the early eighteenth century. The last time the power to refuse Royal Assent was used in the UK was when Queen Anne objected in 1707 to a Bill settling the militia in Scotland. However, we know that King George V contemplated not giving assent to Irish Home Rule in 1914, and Queen Victoria similarly questioned whether she could veto an Irish Home Rule Bill in 1893. In the same year she raised the question of her position in relation to Welsh Disestablishment. More recently the issue of Royal Assent arose in Belgium in 1990 when, as a matter of personal conscience, King Baudouin felt he could not sign an abortion bill. The solution adopted was that the King stood down for a day in order to avoid signing the bill. The law was promulgated by the Cabinet and in an emergency session legislators voted the next day to restore the King to his throne.

In the UK the power of the Head of State to refuse consent to legislation is still real, even if it is not in practice used. Over the last fifty years the UK has had a monarch who has maintained a scrupulous political neutrality, so much so that almost nothing is known of the Queen's political views. But there is no guarantee that such political neutrality will be maintained under every succeeding monarch. Rather unusually the present heir to the throne has made his political views very well known, both in public speeches and in private letters to government ministers, some of which have been publicised. It must be presumed that a future King Charles III would not wish to remain politically assertive in the same way, but his past views at least will remain on the record. This may give rise to certain anxieties if and when legislation is enacted in areas where he has previously expressed strong opinions.

It is not impossible, for example, to envisage future circumstances in which Parliament legislates on issues concerned with, say, genetic manipulation or human cloning, and fears are then expressed that the monarch's personal moral convictions may make it difficult for him to give royal assent. Indeed Article 9 of the Human Rights Act 1998 may give future monarchs the right to refuse Royal Assent on an issue of conscience, although this seems unlikely. Similarly, a crisis over royal assent might be generated by proposals for Scottish independence. If the Scots chose to secede from the UK, the monarch's assent to such a law might be conceived as breaking his or her Coronation Oath, placing the sovereign in a very difficult position, and exposing the continued difficulties of the current settlement.

These scenarios are of course hypothetical and do not reflect the current situation which appears to work perfectly satisfactorily. However, it seems to us preferable that a possible constitutional eventuality should be resolved before, not when, it becomes a problem. This could be achieved by the introduction of a mechanism in statute whereby, if the Head of State's assent is not given directly, it is deemed to have been given seven days after a Bill completes all its Parliamentary stages. This would remove the possibility of a monarch being required to sign legislation which he or she found unacceptable for whatever reason, while the seven day interval would retain an opportunity for action in any crisis such as the attempted enactment of unconstitutional laws.

The ceremonial role

The symbolic aspects of the monarchy's place within the constitution, and in relation to Parliament in particular, raise further questions. Clearly, it is wholly appropriate for the Head of State to retain a symbolic place within the governance of the state, and in the ceremonies and procedures that reflect it. However, the association of modern democratic institutions with excessively archaic rites and symbols can give a very misleading impression of the business of contemporary governance. Where this symbolism signifies the monarch's superiority over the elected Parliament, change is particularly appropriate.

The best known ceremony of this kind is the annual State Opening of Parliament at which the Queen's Speech, setting out the Government's legislative agenda for the session, is delivered. The lavish pageantry of the State Opening is a colourful feature of the constitutional calendar, and it serves to recognise the important relationship between the Head of State and Parliament. Yet its contradictory rituals are highly symbolic of the problem in the relationship between monarch and

Parliament. The rebuff of Black Rod, signifying Parliamentary sovereignty – or at least obstinacy – is juxtaposed with the absurdity of elected Members of Parliament having to stand at the back of the House of Lords during the Queen's Speech.

The overlaying of extreme historicism onto the democratic business of Parliament – of which the State Opening is the prime example – makes for an unhelpful symbolism at a time when democratic institutions are already suffering low public esteem. There is a real risk that attempts to modernise and further democratise Parliament – and the country in turn – are impeded by such associations, confusing a working legislature with a museum. The presentation of the Government's legislative pro-gramme by the Head of State in the Queen's Speech is particu-larly inappropriate. It is the Government's programme, not that of the monarch, and the absurd sight of the Queen making a political speech does a disservice to both institutions.

To address these issues, we believe that reform is needed in both the form and frequency of the State Opening ceremony. First, we see no reason for the State Opening of Parliament to occur every year. It should take place only at the start of a Parliament, not annually, and the proroguing ceremony should be abandoned altogether. Second, the Queen's speech should be replaced by an address by the Head of State relevant to the occa-sion of the opening of a new democratic Parliament. This could be a formal restatement of democratic principle or could be more personal, along the lines of the Christmas Message. The legislative programme should then be presented at a separate session by the Prime Minister and should be debated in accor-dance with normal parliamentary procedure.

Two other areas of parliamentary procedure reflect the sym-bolic derivation of the authority of Parliament, as well as the executive, from the Crown. These are the Parliamentary Oath of Allegiance taken by MPs, and the Humble Address, which requires Parliament to ask the monarch's permission before it can debate issues relating directly to him or her. Both the Oath and the Humble Address reinforce the symbolic subservience of the elected Parliament to the unelected Crown. Both restrict the scope of debate on the constitution within Parliament.

While the historic origins of the Oath and the Humble Address are important, we do not believe that it is appropriate for a modern Parliament to be constrained in this way. The principle should be that Parliament is elected by and for the people. The convention of the Humble Address should simply be removed, providing an implicit assertion of the right of Parliament to debate any issue. The present wording of the Oath of Allegiance is similarly inappropriate and in need of review. This review should seek a form of words that better reflects the public service commitment of those who take it, rather than their allegiance to the office of Head of State.

The law

The position of a serving Head of State in relation to the law is exceptional in most countries, as the protection of the office and its holder makes completely equal treatment with other citizens impossible. This is also the case in the UK.

Immunity of the monarch in almost all respects is the legal starting point, but these immunities have been eroded by statute and by practice in a number of rather complex ways. In principle it was a maxim of the common law that 'The King can do no wrong'. His person was inviolable and immune from all suits and actions at law, either civil or criminal, and no remedy lay against him. No proceeding was maintainable against the sovereign because the courts were his own and they could have no jurisdiction over him.

These rules continue to apply to the sovereign in his or her private capacity, although the Crown Proceedings Act 1947 allowed the Crown (in practice, a Government Department or Minister) to be sued directly in civil proceedings. A number of other express statutory exceptions and practice have complicated the position further. For example, the monarch cannot give evidence in his or her own cause, and it is not clear whether a monarch's evidence is admissible to facts within his or her knowledge. Such evidence may however be received in evidence in civil cases between third parties, and the sovereign may sue in the courts. Constitutional lawyer Professor Sir William

Wade argues that in practice the traditional practice of waiver of immunity and submission to the courts by the sovereign would come into play if he or she were sued or if her evidence were required, and that the monarch would act first and foremost in the interests of justice, of which she is formally the fount, however unseemly or embarrassing the proceedings might be.[4]

These complexities, and the public concern that arise from them, were revealed in stark relief by the Burrell case in the autumn of 2002. Paul Burrell, previously butler to the Princess of Wales, was charged with stealing her property. Before Burrell took the witness stand, the Queen herself came forward (through the Prince of Wales) to say she remembered being told by Burrell that he planned to retain certain items for safe keeping. The trial then collapsed. The case for reviewing the legal position of the Head of State consequently gained a much higher public profile.

It is usual for serving Heads of State to be immune from prosecution. All seven monarchs of European Union states have this immunity. The German Federal President, like the US President, can be impeached but not prosecuted while in office. The Swedish monarch is, in theory, liable to be sued personally in the civil courts, although we understand that this has never occurred in practice.

We see no difficulty in allowing claims to be brought in respect of any civil wrong committed by the monarch personally, possibly with the Attorney General being substituted as defendant. Criminal prosecution is more difficult. Although we are instinctively against immunities and similar privileges, the ban on prosecuting serving heads of state is well established across the world and we do not recommend its removal. In the highly improbable event of a monarch committing a serious offence and refusing to abdicate the monarchy would be unlikely to survive.

On the question of competence to give evidence, the Head of State should be competent to give evidence in court but no defendant should be able to compel him or her to appear as a witness. As already suggested, the Burrell affair has raised public concerns in this respect. In many European countries a serving Head of State cannot be compelled to give evidence. This is a perfectly understandable position as for every reasonable court case there would no doubt be many more examples where people attempted to summon the monarch to court for no good reason. This protection for the Head of State does not ultimately disadvantage defendants. Using the recent Burrell case as an example, if summoning the Queen had genuinely been the only way for Burrell to build his defence he would have been acquitted, since otherwise the Human Rights Act 1998 would have been infringed. However, by ensuring that the Head of State is competent to give evidence, difficulties in similarly sensitive cases could be avoided.

Another reform which should be considered is largely symbolic in its effects, but is important nevertheless. It has already been noted that the British Head of State is seen as above the law, and this is particularly reinforced by the fact that prosecutions are conducted in the name of the Queen. The impression that this gives is in stark contrast to the USA, where prosecutions are conducted in the name of the People. For this reason, we believe it appropriate for prosecutions to be made in the name of the Director of Public Prosecutions, rather than the Queen.

Conclusion

The Head of State is an essential part of our constitutional settlement, performing an important role in our system of government. Yet for the needs of a modern democracy, the existing arrangements are ill-defined and leave too great a degree of political discretion for an unelected office. The argument that these powers are seldom used, much less abused, is often deployed to counter pressure for reform. The system works, it is argued, and should be left alone. However, the current arrangements leave open the possibility of problems in the future, and in these circumstances it is highly desirable that they are dealt with now rather than at a time of crisis. If the rationale for retaining these powers is that they are never used, it is difficult to see why their reform should be opposed.

Over and above the specific powers dealt with in this chapter, we believe that reform is needed in order to define clearly the office of Head of State. The current informal nature of the office, based on custom, practice and convention, and tied so closely to the Royal Family, leaves too much for interpretation and is too bound up with the personality of its incumbent. We do not believe that this is compatible with a modern democracy. At a time of major constitutional change in other areas, the constitutional position of the Head of State is too important to leave so ill-defined.

Notes

1   *The Monarchy and the Constitution*, Vernon Bogdanor, OUP 1995

2   *The Nature of the Crown*, Maurice Sunkin and Sebastian Payne (eds), OUP 1999

3   Bogdanor, *op. cit.*

4   *The Times*, 27th November 2002

Chapter 5

The Head of State and the Anglican Church

In common with some other constitutional monarchies in Europe, the British Head of State has a a close relationship with organised religion – or rather, with one particular denomination. The monarchy is formally tied to the Church of England, and has a much looser involvement in the Church of Scotland.

These relationships are in part symbolic, in part institutional. At a ceremonial level, the very authority of the office is held to come from the divine rather than the democratic, a symbolism reflected in the Coronation ceremony and Oath. It is the Archbishop of Canterbury who places the crown on the new sovereign's head, and the monarch in return swears to defend the Church of England.[1] But there is also an institutional integration between the Head of State and the established Church. The monarch is constitutionally the Supreme Governor of the Church of England and it is he or she who appoints the Church of England's bishops. The very legislation of the Church is ultimately governed by the state.

For most of the last 450 years the establishment of the Church of England and its intertwining with the British state reflected a nation the majority of whose population were members of the Anglican Church. But times change and the religious make-up of the UK is now very different. How far is it tenable for one faith and one denomination to maintain this institutional primacy through its links to the Head of State, an office which is meant to represent the whole nation? In a modern democracy, is divine authority – albeit symbolic – consistent with an otherwise secular system of government? This chapter will explore the institutional relationships between the state, the Head of State and the

Church of England, and will ask whether those relationships can represent more effectively the Britain of the twenty-first century. To do this we need first to understand exactly what those relationships are.

The established Church

The UK is not the only country where the Head of State is formally linked to a particular faith. Three other European monarchs – those of Sweden, Denmark and Norway – are constitutionally bound to profess the state religion. The monarchs of Luxembourg, Spain, the Netherlands, Belgium, Monaco and Liechtenstein are not subject to any religious restrictions.

The institutional relationship between the Head of State and the Church of England has two dimensions. First, the relationship is enshrined within the Act of Settlement of 1701[2] which stipulates that only Protestant descendants of Princess Sophia are eligible to succeed to the throne and disbars any heir who marries a Catholic. This is reinforced after the accession of each new monarch through the Coronation Oath, in which the sovereign also swears to defend the Anglican Church.

The second institutional relationship is through the establishment of the Church of England. This comprises three discrete elements. The monarch has the title and position of Supreme Governor of the Church of England. He or she appoints, on the advice of senior church leaders, the bishops of the Church, and the senior bishops sit in the House of Lords. Church legislation has to be ratified by Parliament, although discretion over these powers has been devolved to the General Synod since the early 20th century.

While the Church of England is in this way established and linked to the UK's Head of State, this does not apply to any of the other Anglican churches within the UK – those of Scotland, Wales and Ireland. In Wales and Ireland the Church is fully disestablished; in Scotland, the Church occupies an intermediate position as the 'national ' church, although the institutional ties with the state and the Head of State are much weaker. In no other Anglican Church, including those in Commonwealth countries where the British monarch is also the Head of State, does the Church have this kind of formal relationship.

Supreme Governor

The UK's Head of State is also the Supreme Governor of the Church of England. This title was established by Henry VIII's Act of Supremacy of 1532, which states that the monarch is Supreme Governor 'in all spiritual and ecclesiastical things and causes'. (He or she is not, however, formally the head of the church – this position is reserved for Christ.) It is this royal supremacy which distinguishes the Church of England from the status of most churches as associations based upon mutual contract, and in particular from most of the continental Protestant churches in which authority is held to lie in the scriptures, not in any mortal individual.

The Preface to the 39 Articles of the Church of England describes the sovereign as 'being by God's Ordinance, according to Our Just Title, Defender of the Faith and Supreme Governor of the Church of England'. The monarch must be a full, confirmed member of the Church of England and, in his or her Coronation Oath, the monarch promises 'to maintain and preserve inviolably' the Church. Article 37 declares that as Supreme Governor of the Church of England, the monarch:

'...hath the chief power in this Realm of England, and other his Dominions, unto whom the chief Government of all Estates of this Realm, whether they be Ecclesiastical or Civil, in all causes doth appertain, and is not, nor ought to be, subject to any foreign jurisdiction.' [3]

The Supreme Governorship is not just a Church position. It is a constitutional one which the sovereign occupies by virtue of his or her position as Head of State, from which it cannot be separated. There is no other qualification for the position of Supreme Governor, and the personal beliefs and behaviour of the sovereign are irrelevant to it.

Appointment of bishops

As Supreme Governor the monarch appoints archbishops and bishops on the advice of the Prime Minister, who considers the names selected by a Church body. Bishops, on appointment, take an oath of allegiance to the reigning monarch and may not resign without royal authority. Parish priests also take an oath of allegiance. In the past the Church had even less autonomy over its own appointments. Until 1976 the Prime Minister had an unfettered right to advise the Queen on appointments, and the Church had no formal role in the process at all, although it was consulted as a matter of courtesy. Since 1976 the Church's role has been formalised; appointments are now submitted to the Prime Minister through the Church of England's Crown Appointments Commission, a body of which a majority is made up of members of the Synod. This Commission presents a short-list of two, which may be in order of preference, for the Prime Minister to consider. Once the Prime Minister has made a decision, he or she submits it to the Queen for approval.

The intertwining of Church and state goes further. The Archbishops of Canterbury and York, the Bishops of London, Durham, and Winchester, and twenty-one other diocesan bishops in order of seniority sit in the House of Lords. These positions were not affected by the Labour Government's House of Lords Act 1999, which abolished the right of most hereditary peers to sit in the upper house. Since the House of Commons (Removal of Clergy Disqualification) Act 2001, ordained members of the Church of England have been permitted to sit in the House of Commons, from which they had previously been prohibited.

Church legislation

Power over the legislation of the Church of England formally rests with Parliament. Since The Church of England Assembly (Powers) Act of 1919, however, it has been devolved to the General Synod (formerly the Church Assembly). The 1919 Act gave the Synod the power to pass Measures relating to Church matters. Before these become law they must be approved by both Houses of Parliament and then submitted for Royal Assent. Parliament cannot amend or initiate Measures, or discuss Church matters. Parliament has a power of veto on Measures, though this in effect is more like the House of Lords' power to delay legislation than a true power of veto, and it is rarely used. However, Measures may amend or repeal Acts of Parliament.

The Synod also has the power to make Canons that bind only the clergy. These do not require Parliamentary approval but are submitted directly to the monarch for the Royal Licence to promulgate, typically acting on ministerial advice. Theoretically, the Head of State has the power to veto Canons, although this has never actually happened. However, they have on occasion been withdrawn before being presented in cases where it was felt the Home Secretary would advise their veto.

The 1919 Act was followed in 1974 by the Church of England (Worship and Doctrine) Measure, which repealed much of the Act of Uniformity of 1662 (which required all ministers to assent to the rites and liturgy of the Established Church) and delegated further power to the Synod. The trend in this area is clearly towards greater delegation. This is due in part to a desire among Church leaders for greater independence, but also to the acknowledgement among Members of Parliament that, with fewer and fewer of them being members of the Church of England, Parliament can no longer claim any legitimate authority in ecclesiastical matters.

The Churches of Scotland, Wales and Ireland

The institutional relationship between the Head of State and the Anglican Church is firmly rooted. However, it is not uniform across the four branches of Anglicanism across the UK, and there are distinct arrangements in Scotland, Wales and Ireland.

Under the Union with Scotland Act 1707, the monarch has a duty to 'maintain and preserve inviolably' both the Church of England and the Church of Scotland. While both these churches are national churches and are established in that they are singled out in statute, the Church of Scotland is entirely self-governing. Having been granted the power to determine matters of worship, doctrine and discipline in the Church of Scotland Act 1921, the Church of Scotland, unlike that of England, is independent from, and not subordinate to, the state.

The Churches of Wales and Ireland are still further removed, being now fully disestablished. Throughout the nineteenth century the establishment of both was increasingly anomalous, not least because these were minority churches, with the majority of people in Ireland being members of the Roman Catholic Church and the majority in Wales adhering to the Free Churches. The Irish Church Act of 1869 dissolved the statutory union between the Churches of England and Ireland and disestablished the Irish Church entirely. A General Synod was created in 1890 and given legislative and administrative power. In Wales disestablishment was enacted in 1914 although this did not come into force until 1920. In many ways this was a very radical reform, as the then four Welsh dioceses were an organic part of the Church of England.

Faith in the UK

The institutional relationships between the monarchy and the Church of England are very powerful. Yet how strong is the connection between the Church of England and the population of the UK? How far does this intertwining of Church and state represent the nation?

It is often said that Britain is no longer a religious country. It is also sometimes claimed that the Church of England, even among the religious, is now a minority faith. The facts are rather more complex than this. Yet they do broadly support the view that the institutional primacy of the Church of England within the state can no longer be justified solely on the grounds of its primacy in the country.

In the 2001 Census, 37 million people (nearly 72 per cent) gave their religion as Christian – clearly a substantial majority. The second largest faith in Britain is Islam, with 1.5 million followers (3 per cent of the population). The British include 552,000 Hindus, 329,000 Sikhs, 260,000 Jews, and 144,000 Buddhists. Those actively identifying themselves as holding no religion numbered 7.7 million (15 per cent), a substantial minority, but a minority nonetheless.[4] The British, therefore, remain predominantly Christian. Of these, around 24 million are members of the Church of England with around 700,000 members of the Church of Scotland and 100,000 members of the Church of Wales. There are six million Roman Catholics, as well as a number of other Christian denominations such as Orthodox, Methodist and Pentecostal.

These figures however relate to church 'membership' in its widest sense of identification. The number of people who can be considered active church members is far fewer. Surveys suggest that there are no more than around 1.1 million people (around 2.6 per cent of the population) who regularly attend Anglican services, compared to 1.3 million who attend Roman Catholic services, and 1.2 million attending the independent Protestant churches.[5] So while the Church of England can claim that a large number of British citizens identify with it as the national church, the religious meaning of that identification is less clear. Britain is probably less religious in this sense than at any point in its post-medieval history, and – perhaps most importantly – among those British citizens for whom religion is an active part of their lives, a majority are not Anglican.

In Chapter 2 we argued that the role of the monarchy as a unifying symbol in society was an important strength. However, as we argued in Chapter 3, to fulfil this role effectively the institution needs to be as representative as possible. As Britain becomes more multicultural and multi-faith, the close and formal association of the monarchy with one denomination tends to undermine this principle. Clearly, no single holder of any position can be representative of a diverse country in him or herself. With a hereditary principle, representativeness is also unlikely to be achieved over time through the personal characteristics of the office holder, since successive monarchs are likely to be of the same faith. Sociologists therefore describe the need for a Head of State to be 'existentially representative' – the office must transcend the characteristics of its individual incumbents and embody the concept of national representation. By this is meant that, for example, even though no member of the royal family is a Sikh, a British Sikh person should nevertheless feel represented by the monarchy.

Given the range of religious faiths practised in Britain today there is, we believe, a genuine question over whether the current relationship between the monarch and the Church of England is conducive to this aim of existential representation. The Prince of Wales himself has shown an awareness of this issue:

'I've always felt that the Catholic subjects of the sovereign are equally as important as the Anglican ones, as the Protestant ones. Likewise, I think that the Islamic subjects or the Hindu subjects or the Zoroastrian subjects of the sovereign are of equal and vital importance.'[6]

Indeed Charles went further, declaring that he would wish to be seen as King to be a 'Defender of Faith', rather than the 'Defender of the Faith' (namely, Anglicanism) required by the Coronation Oath. This is not incompatible with being a member of the Church of England but it does recognise the multi-faith character of the nation of which he will be sovereign. More recently he has said that he would like his coronation to be an inter-faith occasion,[7] similar, for example, to the D-day commemorations of 1994, in which non-Anglican faiths were invited to participate. However, desirable as though this might be, it does not address the question of the representation of the growing number of Britons who hold no faith. In turn this raises questions about the formal and ceremonial religious content of the office of Head of State, regardless of faith and denomination.

Our conclusion is that there are some areas of the relationship between the monarch and the Church of England which could be reformed. The aim of such reforms should be to increase the representativeness of the office of Head of State and – as part of this – to remove the historical prejudice of the bar on Catholics succeeding and marrying into the royal family.

Distancing the Church and state

If the Head of State is to perform the role of unifying the diverse communities of the UK, and to act as the representative of contemporary Britain, we believe that Church and state need to be distanced, both symbolically and institutionally.

One possible model for such distancing might be that of the Church of Scotland, which has a weaker institutional relationship to the Head of State. The monarch has no role as Supreme Governor but is bound to support the Church by oath, and sends a High Commissioner to attend the General Assembly of the Church. The Commissioner sits in the gallery and takes no part in the proceedings. If this model were to be adopted for the Church of England, the Head of State would cease to be Supreme Governor. It would then be possible to have a Head of State who was not a member of the Church of England, or even not a Christian, without disrupting the business of the Church. However, while the Church of Scotland model would deal with the technical problems associated with reform of the Act of Settlement, it would not address the issue of representation, because there would remain an institutional link between the Church and State. The Church would continue to have constitutional primacy.

We therefore believe that at least some measure of disestablishment is necessary to ensure the proper representativeness of the office of Head of State. A continuing close and formal relationship between the Head of State and any one faith – or indeed with organised religion of any kind – is no longer appropriate for modern Britain. It is notable that, of the four constituent nations of the UK, it is only in England that the Anglican Church enjoys this position. Indeed, of the 38 worldwide provinces of the Anglican Church, only the Church of England is established in this way.

Disestablishment of the Church of England is usually spoken of as if it were an all or nothing choice. In fact it is quite possible to separate the three constituent elements that make up the establishment of the Church. As we have seen, these are the monarch's role as Supreme Governor, the appointment of bishops and their position in the House of Lords, and the parliamentary control of Church legislation.

Of these, only the ending of the monarch's role as Supreme Governor is critical to the aim of representativeness. It is this requirement of the institution which underpins the Catholic bar in the Act of Settlement – since the Head of State is the Church of England's Supreme Governor, a Catholic could not be allowed on the throne. Logically, though not in law, it also disbars anyone of any other faith. Ending the constitutional role of Supreme Governor would therefore enable both the Catholic bar on succession, and the prohibition on Catholic marriages in the 1701 Act of Succession, to be repealed.

There are clearly good reasons why the other elements of establishment should be examined. But they are not primarily issues concerning the role of Head of State, and are therefore beyond the remit of this report. The process of appointment of bishops and the control of Church legislation are matters of church governance which should be decided in our view by the Church of England itself. Many will ask why the Church should wish to be dependent on the state to govern itself, but this is a matter for it, not for outsiders, to change if it so wishes. The position of bishops in the House of Lords relates to a different constitutional issue, the structure of the upper house, and should be considered as part of that reform process. But none of these changes are necessary for the reform which most concerns us here. In this sense, disestablishment can be partial.

One of the objections to disestablishment often made by members of the Church of England is that it would lead to the church becoming a 'sect', serving only its active churchgoers rather than the wider community (including those of other faiths and no faith) which it now sees as its constituency. The basis for the establishment of the Church was the Tudor synchrony of the Protestant congregation and English citizenry. And the Church's leading role in contemporary national life still owes as much to its resources and its universal geographic coverage as to its formal establishment. Through its parochial structure the Church of England encompasses the whole country, with around 98 per cent of those considered by the Church to be its parishioners not actively linked to Anglicanism.[8] None of this, however, would disappear were the position of Supreme Governor to be ended. In this sense the Church of England would remain the 'national' Church; only its formal links to the Head of State would have been abolished.

A second reason why many leaders of the Church have in the past supported the retention of its established status is that they believe it provides a formal place for faith within, and therefore moral content to, politics.[9] We are not convinced, however, that such influence and voice would cease just because the Church had been disentangled from the state. The moral authority of the Archbishop of Canterbury does not derive from his links to the monarchy or the fact that he sits in the House of Lords. It relates to his position as head of the largest church in the nation, a church with coverage in all parts of the country, as well as to his own personal qualities of probity and wisdom. Given the diversity of religious belief in Britain today we see no reason why leaders of other faiths, as well as those with no faith, should not share the responsibility of providing a moral framework for public and political discourse.

Disestablishment of the Church of England, whether full or partial, does not in any way require a Head of State to give up his or her own faith or involvement in religious organisations. Indeed, a monarch might choose to be a patron of one or more faiths – or none – in the same way that members of the royal family currently choose to be patrons of other civil institutions. However, the involvement of a Head of State in this way should clearly not indicate a formal religious role for the office, nor a primacy for any one faith within the institutions of the state.

Ian Bradley has argued that in part the strong popular identification of the Crown with the Church is due to the Queen's involvement in occasions of a religious nature such as Remembrance Sunday and the Christmas broadcast.[10] However this arises from her capacity as Head of State, not as Supreme Governor. So we do not believe that ending the association of the two roles would adversely impact upon such activities.

If the constitutional relationship of the Head of State with the Church of England is ended, it would be sensible for the same to occur to the already weaker relationship with the Church of Scotland.

The Accession and the Coronation

If the monarch's role as Supreme Governor of the Church of England represents the key institutional link between the Head of State and the Church, the most visible symbolic representation of the relationship is the Coronation. Though often thought of as the occasion when the new monarch formally accedes to the throne, and therefore as the moment of constitutional transition, the Coronation is actually a religious service, not primarily a constitutional one. It takes place about a year after formal accession – which occurs at a different (and much less well known) ceremony on the death of the previous sovereign. The Coronation ceremony is conducted not by a secular public figure but by the Archbishop of Canterbury, head of the Church, who anoints the sovereign and delivers the Orb, the symbol of sovereignty, to the new monarch. The ceremony includes the religious rite of Holy Communion, and in the Coronation Oath the monarch swears to maintain the Church. In all these ways the Coronation as historically defined confirms the essentially religious character of the position of British Head of State. As the theologian P Avis observes, in the Coronation:

'...the Sovereign is seen as answerable to a higher power. Crowned and consecrated by the archbishops and bishops of the Church of England, she exercises her office as a duty and privilege that comes from God... Crown, Church and constitution are bound up together in a delicate ecology.'[11]

This does not imply that the Coronation cannot have secular meaning too, as a great public event observed by the nation together. Analysing the 1953 Coronation in the *Sociological Review*, Edward Shils and Michael Young described it as:

'...the ceremonial occasion for the affirmation of the moral values by which the society lives. It was an act of national communion.'[12]

But its primary content concerns the divine authority of the sovereign. Ian Bradley notes that:

'In Christian coronations, the focus was not on choosing a king or even crowning and enthroning him, but rather on invoking the divine blessing, setting him apart and reminding him of the derivation of his power from God and of his responsibilities to rule wisely, justly and mercifully.'[13]

Central to this purpose is the Coronation Oath. The monarch swears to do her utmost to:

'...maintain the Laws of God and the true profession of the Gospel... maintain in the United Kingdom the Protestant Reformed Religion established by law... maintain and preserve inviolably the settlement of the Church of England, and the doctrine, worship, discipline, and gov-

ernment thereof, as by law established in England... preserve unto the Bishops and Clergy of England, and to the Churches there committed to their charge, all such rights and privileges, as by law do or shall appertain to them or any of them '[14]

The religious character of the institution could hardly be made clearer. In fact, some church authorities claim that the Coronation Oath in some way imparts Christian authority not just to the monarchy but to the other institutions of the state too. Ian Bradley cites *The Bulletin of the National Council for Christian Standards* as saying:

'The remarkable thing is that Britain, through leaders in past generations, set out to be, as a nation, in Covenant with Almighty God. The pivot of the Covenants is the Coronation Oath, which is based on the intention that all the institutions of the nation are to be governed according to the laws of God.' [15]

The religious character of the Coronation ceremony confirms the historic entwinement of the Head of State and the Church. Perhaps more surprising is that there is no ceremony at which the new monarch swears an oath to serve the nation as Head of State at all.

The transfer of sovereign powers to a new monarch is made immediately upon the death of his or her predecessor. The formal proclamation of accession is made at an Accession Council held in St James's Palace. To this are invited the Privy Council, members of the House of Lords, High Commissioners of Commonwealth countries and some others – but not the elected Members of Parliament. In the case of Elizabeth II, the Accession Council took place at the Court at St. James's, on 8th February 1952, where the new Queen made a declaration and signed the Accession document. The new monarch then swears an oath, known as the Royal Declaration, at the next State Opening of Parliament. This oath is the formal public declaration by the new monarch, and since 1910[16] it has run:

'I do solemnly and sincerely in the presence of God, profess, testify, and declare that I am a faithful Protestant, and that I will, according to the true intent of the enactments to secure the Protestant Succession to the Throne of my realm, uphold and maintain such enactments to the best of my power.' [17]

This declaration is required in order to uphold the Act of Succession. Again, it clearly places the connection between Head of State and the Church at its centre. In fact, no part of the Accession ceremony or Royal Declaration involves an oath of service as Head of State of the kind sworn by almost every other Head of State in the modern world.

Reforming the Accession and Coronation

The Coronation and Accession ceremonies are historic traditions – though by no means unchanged over time. But they are also important occasions in the constitutional life of the UK, and therefore in helping to define the nation's sense of itself. We do not believe that their centrally and specifically Anglican character is now appropriate for a modern Britain of many faiths and none. We believe that the ceremonies at which a new Head of State takes office need to reflect and represent the nation he or she is being asked to serve.

The more important ceremony in this regard is the Accession, rather than the Coronation. It is at the Accession that the new monarch takes office as Head of State. We believe that for this reason the Accession ceremony should be made secular, democratic, and public. It is not our place to design such a ceremony but it seems to us that it should be, and look, as representative of modern Britain as possible, with those attending coming from every part of the national community. It should include the involvement of the elected representatives of the people – Members of Parliament – and its symbolic focus should be on the democratic authority conferred on the monarch as Head of State. It might be appropriate in this respect for the ceremony to be conducted by a senior figure from the secular institutions of the constitution such as the Speaker of the House of Commons or the Lord Chief Justice. In the Accession declaration or oath the new Head of State should then, in some form, swear to serve the people of the UK and to uphold its constitution and laws.

Interestingly, despite its pageantry, the Coronation is not a fixed ceremony and historically has been open to change. If, as we propose, the Accession is made into the proper legal inauguration of the Head of State, there is no reason why the

Coronation should not remain essentially a blessing and a celebration. As such the ceremony could reflect the faith, if any, of the incoming monarch, or, as Prince Charles has suggested, could involve all faiths – or indeed have no religious content. The Coronation Oath itself, however, should be redrafted to be properly secular, again based on an undertaking to serve the people. There is every reason for the ceremony to be flexible and to reflect the character of the times and of the incoming sovereign. There is certainly no reason why the pageantry of the occasion – which provides much of its public appeal – should be lost. On the contrary, the pageantry confirms the Coronation as a ceremony of celebration. As such, again, it is important to ensure that it is representative in content and appearance. The investiture of a new Head of State is a moment for the whole nation, and the whole nation should have the opportunity of feeling represented by it.

Notes

1 *God Save the Queen*, Ian Bradley, Darton, Longman and Todd 2000

2 Act of Settlement 1701, reprinted in *English Historical Documents 1660-1714*, Andrew Browning (ed), 1953

3 39 Articles, 1571

4 The question on religion was voluntary and just over four million people chose not to answer it

5 Taken from the 2001 UK Census, published 8th May 2003, and the Guardian website www.guardian.co.uk/religion/

6 *The Prince of Wales*, Jonathan Dimbleby, Littlebrown 1994

7 The *Observer*, 26th January 2003

8 According to the Church of England's figures, Church Statistics 2000, 1,058,000 people attend services each Sunday

9 Colin Buchanan, Bishop of Woolwich, in oral evidence presented to the Commission, 14th November 2002

10 Bradley *op. cit.*

11 *ibid.*

12 *ibid.*

14 Order of Service for the Coronation

15 Bradley, *op. cit.*

16 Between 1689 and 1910, the Royal Declaration ran as follows: 'I, A. B., by the grace of God King (or Queen) of England, Scotland and Ireland, Defender of the Faith, do solemnly and sincerely in the presence of God, profess, testify, and declare, that I do believe that in the Sacrament of the Lord's Supper there is not any Transubstantiation of the elements of bread and wine into the Body and Blood of Christ at or after the consecration thereof by any person whatsoever: and that the invocation or adoration of the Virgin Mary or any other Saint, and the Sacrifice of the Mass, as they are now used in the Church of Rome, are superstitious and idolatrous. And I do solemnly in the presence of God profess, testify, and declare that I do make this declaration, and every part thereof, in the plain and ordinary sense of the words read unto me, as they are commonly understood by English Protestants, without any such dispensation from any person or authority or person whatsoever, or without thinking that I am or can be acquitted before God or man, or absolved of this declaration or any part thereof, although the Pope, or any other person or persons, or power whatsoever, should dispense with or annul the same or declare that it was null and void from the beginning.'

17 Accession Declaration Act, 1910

Chapter 6

The Head of State and the Commonwealth

The link between the British monarchy and the Commonwealth is bound up with the history of both. The Commonwealth emerged in the postwar period from the transition to independence of the countries of the British Empire. This has given Queen Elizabeth II two different kinds of institutional role. She is the Head of the Commonwealth, a formal position in the international organisation. But she is also Queen and Head of State of fifteen of its member countries in addition to the UK.

It is well known that these roles have remained very important to the Queen, so much so that it is sometimes hard to determine where the institutional relationships end and the personal ones begin. In fact it is true to say that the roles are quite individual to the Queen herself; their relatively recent origin means that they cannot properly be said to be aspects of her constitutional position as the British Head of State. In this chapter we examine these roles and how they might develop in future.

The Commonwealth and its Head

The Commonwealth of Nations is a voluntary association of 54 sovereign states, bound together originally through the British Empire. It declares itself to be an association of equals and aims to advance democracy, human rights and sustainable economic and social development within its member countries and beyond.[1]

Most of the members are republics, with only sixteen – including the UK – retaining the British monarch as their Head of State (see box on opposite page). More accurately, these sixteen countries retain their own monarch, who is also the British monarch, a distinction we shall return to below. A further four countries are monarchies under separate royal families; the remainder are governed by other systems.

Constitutional Arrangements of Commonwealth Countries

Constitutional monarchies under Elizabeth II
Antigua and Barbuda, Australia, The Bahamas, Barbados, Belize, Canada, Grenada, Jamaica, Mauritius, New Zealand, Papua New Guinea, Saint Christopher and Nevis, Saint Vincent and the Grenadines, The Solomon Islands, Tuvalu and the United Kingdom.

Republics
Bangladesh, Botswana, Cyprus, Dominica, The Gambia, Ghana, Guyana, India, Kenya, Kiribati, Malawi, Maldives, Malta, Mozambique, Nauru, Nigeria, Pakistan, Seychelles, Sierra Leone, Singapore, Sri Lanka, Tanzania, Trinidad and Tobago, Uganda, Vanuatu, Zambia and Zimbabwe.

Other arrangements
Of the remaining members, Lesotho, Malaysia, Swaziland and Tonga are monarchies, Brunei is a sultanate, and Western Samoa elects a Paramount Chief as its Head of State.

The Commonwealth gradually evolved as the constituent parts of the British Empire won independence. Originally it had no Head; membership of the Commonwealth was based solely on allegiance to the British Crown. But once India and other countries had become independent as republics, this was no longer tenable. The position of Head of the Commonwealth was created after the London Declaration of 1949, in which India proclaimed its desire to continue as a full member of the Commonwealth and its acceptance of George VI as the symbol of the free association of independent countries. The new formula enabled India and other republics to remain within the organisation.

Following George VI's death in 1952, Queen Elizabeth II was unanimously accepted as Head of the Commonwealth. The position is for life, but it is personal to her; it is not hereditary. There is no Commonwealth rule that the next British monarch will succeed to the position. Within the Commonwealth the position of Head has no constitutional or executive functions: it is simply a symbolic focus for the organisation. However over the last fifty years Elizabeth II has made the position into a substantive and important one. It is widely recognised that, as she began to travel within the Commonwealth, she became particularly conscious of the importance of preserving it through turbulent times. During the upheavals of the unilateral declaration of independence in Rhodesia, apartheid in South Africa, Idi Amin's rule in Uganda and the more recent suspensions of Zimbabwe and Pakistan, the Queen as Head of the Commonwealth has been widely seen as a stabilising influence. It is almost entirely under her stewardship that the development of the organisation has taken place, and it is widely felt that her commitment to it has enhanced its reputation and profile.

Richard Bourne, Head of the Commonwealth Studies Institute in London, argues that the Queen's personal interest in and knowledge of the Commonwealth and its member countries have enabled her to turn what was originally a purely symbolic role into something more substantive:

'Objective observers would say that the Queen has shown a serious understanding of the contemporary value of the Commonwealth, even though the Headship itself is perhaps more popular in Africa and the Caribbean than it is in South Asia. This understanding has been particularly important when presidents, prime ministers and media have forgotten or denigrated the Commonwealth.' [2]

The Queen's formal role has perhaps been most visible in opening the summit meetings of Commonwealth heads of government. There has been a recent shift in the nature of that involvement. Until 1997, the Queen visited the host country, gave a banquet and, throughout the course of the meeting, received the heads of government. However, in order to stress the non-political nature of her role the Queen did not open the summit meeting itself and often left the host country soon after it began. This changed in 1997 at the summit in Edinburgh, at which the Queen gave a short speech to open the heads of government meeting, a precedent which has been followed since. In addition to the summits, the Queen maintains close links with the Commonwealth through regular contact with the organisation's Secretary General. She also retains a visible presence in Commonwealth countries, both through her regular visits to them and through events such as the Christmas broadcast, the Commonwealth Day message and the opening and closing ceremonies of the Commonwealth Games.

There is little doubt that for many of the peoples of the Commonwealth the Queen's visits bring a certain glamour. Indeed the contrast between her visits overseas and many of her engagements in the UK has often been noted. Until the Golden Jubilee year it was far more common for the Queen to be photographed in informal settings in Commonwealth countries than in Britain.

The next Head of the Commonwealth

The decision to make the Queen Head of the Commonwealth on the death of her father was in many ways the result of the instant positive reaction felt towards her by India's Prime Minister Jawarhal Nehru. Her succession was not automatic, since this was the first time that one Head had succeeded another. Today the same question arises of whether, at the end of Elizabeth II's reign, the next British monarch should be appointed Head of the Commonwealth on accession to the throne. If he is not, the Commonwealth will either have to appoint a new Head, or change its arrangements altogether.

There are no formal mechanisms for this decision. The task of initiating the process is likely to fall to the Secretary General, who will be expected to consult with the heads of government of member states to see how they wish to proceed. It is possible that the 1952 precedent will be followed with the position being filled by the new King Charles as Elizabeth II's heir. However, while the Queen inherited the position seamlessly from her father, it is not clear that on her death the transition from the Queen to the next Head will be as uncomplicated.

The 1952 transition clearly sets a precedent, but it is not one that can be said to be deeply embedded, since circumstances have not yet arisen for it to be followed. When the decision arises it is possible that Commonwealth leaders will feel that, though a hereditary succession worked well for Elizabeth II, circumstances today are very different from those in 1952, and a different model should now be instituted.

There are several reasons why this might be argued. In the first place it is difficult to separate the position of Head from the person who has held it for all but its first three years. The Queen has developed the role of Head of the Commonwealth into a substantive and personal one. But after her death, when her particular individual presence is gone, it may be decided that there is no longer a place for what is essentially a symbolic title. Commonwealth expert Richard Bourne suggests that the Queen's work:

'...will look to have been a unique contribution and, by then in her absence, a British monarchical Headship could seem an odd arrangement in an association where the great majority of members are republics...It may be that the Commonwealth will have outgrown the need for a ceremonial Head.' [3]

Part of this feeling clearly arises from a sense that an association of 54 independent countries across the world no longer needs a British monarch to bind it together. The British imperial link is long past; indeed, since Mozambique (a former Portuguese colony) joined, the Commonwealth is no longer the exclusive preserve of former British colonies. The British monarch's relationship to the majority of member states has changed. In 1952 only one Commonwealth state was a republic: today fewer than a third retain the Queen as Head of State. It is true that the Commonwealth Secretariat and Institute are in London, but this is mainly a practical arrangement.

But there is another reason why the question of the succession is now being discussed in Commonwealth countries. It relates to the particular position of Prince Charles as heir. For whatever reason, Prince Charles is widely seen in Commonwealth circles as having rather little interest in the institution or its members. It may be that he has seen this as his mother's specialism and role and therefore not an area into which he should tread. But it is certainly true that he has travelled relatively little in the Commonwealth and there is little public evidence that he gives it a high priority among his concerns. In these circumstances – unless these perceptions are changed over the next few years – there is a very real possibility that Commonwealth leaders will not wish to see a hereditary succession to the position of Head.

If this were the case, what then would happen? One possibility is that the position of Head of the Commonwealth would be ended altogether. Having been established in an earlier era, and associated so long with Queen Elizabeth II, it would be seen as no longer necessary to have a symbolic figurehead at all. The Secretary General already provides leadership, and the Commonwealth Secretariat, which did not exist in 1949, gives substance to the association. However, there would certainly be some who would argue that simply replacing the figurehead with the Secretary General might not be sufficient. There remain certain tensions within the Commonwealth, and even an international civil servant with the status of the Secretary General would not have same authority as an elected president or prime minister chairing a meeting of his or her peers. An alternative approach therefore could be to retain the office of Head of the Commonwealth, but to fill it with some other senior figure, perhaps elected for a limited term of office, from the member countries – a former prime minister or president, perhaps. There are a number of distinguished former political leaders who might be regarded as an appropriate figurehead.

A third possibility would be to rotate the position of Head amongst the member states, much as the European Union does its Presidency. If the post were shared amongst heads of state rather than heads of government, this solution would serve to remove the permanence, but not the fact, of the position being filled by the British monarch: the position would frequently be occupied by Britain's King or Queen since he or she is also Head of State of so many other Commonwealth countries.

Alternatively rotation could be effected through expanding the existing role of Chairperson-in-Office, a position created at the 1999 Durban summit. This is occupied by a head of government and has some leadership responsibility from one heads' meeting to the next. However, South African President Mbeki, the first Chair from 1999-2002, made little use of this role other than encouraging the celebration of Commonwealth Day and providing nominal leadership to a review group on the future of the organisation. The position of Chairperson was subtly redefined after the Coolum summit in March 2002 when Australian Prime Minister John Howard took over the post.

The nature and occupant of the role of Head of the Commonwealth is plainly a matter for the member countries and the future of the office will need to be decided collectively. Whichever option is taken, there is clearly a strong case that the decision be made now, some years in advance of its being required. Given the potential for embarrassment and dispute which would follow a precipitate decision to change the current arrangements on the death of the Queen, it would be highly desirable to have the future status of the office consulted on, agreed and announced in a period of calm beforehand.

The Queen as Head of other states

In addition to her position as Head of State of the UK, Elizabeth II is currently also monarch of fifteen other Commonwealth countries, in addition to the remaining British colonies. On her accession in 1952 she was for the first time proclaimed by different titles in the independent 'realms' of the Commonwealth. The Royal Titles Act of 1953 had to reflect the fact that the Commonwealth realms – Commonwealth countries that retained a monarchical constitution, recognising the Queen as Head of State – were full and equal members of the Commonwealth with the UK.

Since India became a republic an increasing number of member countries have chosen a republican system of government and this is now the case in the majority of Commonwealth states. In most African countries, Guyana, Kiribati and Nauru, executive presidencies were created; India, Bangladesh and Trinidad & Tobago have opted for constitutional presidencies. For most of these countries republican status has been an important symbol of independence.

The reasons why some other members of the Commonwealth have been keen to retain the Queen as Head of State vary. In Canada, the Queen is often felt to act as a unifier of tensions between the various provinces and the federal state. In New Zealand, considerable personal fondness towards her appears to have affected constitutional attitudes. In some of the smaller countries the monarchy has been regarded as providing a form of political security, avoiding the need for substantial – and difficult – constitutional change. In general the trend has been towards republicanism in those countries where there is cross-party consensus, and an avoidance of the issue where there is not. In Barbados, Jamaica and Australia, however, serious public debates have been held over recent years. Australia held a referendum on the issue in 1999. Amid highly public disagreements among republicans about what should replace the monarchy, the proposal to replace the Queen as Head of State was lost, but it is generally expected that the issue will resurface at some point in the future. In a number of other countries it is widely anticipated that similar debates will occur after the Queen's death.

The divisible monarchy

There are of course some complications associated with a number of independent countries effectively sharing a Head of State. This is particularly the case where the incumbent is most closely embedded within one of those countries. On a day-to-day basis the Queen acts on the advice of her UK ministers and her expenses are met by the British taxpayer. This could be seen to compromise her legal independence as head of other states.

In fact the status of the monarch is more complex than this. Constitutionally, the monarchy is 'divisible'. By this is meant the Queen of the UK is in law a separate and distinct monarch from the Queen of Australia, from the Queen of Jamaica, and so on. When she visits one of the Commonwealth countries of which she is Head of State she speaks and acts as Queen of that country, not as sovereign of the UK, and she acts on the advice of the ministers of the country concerned.

Outside the UK the Queen is represented by a Governor-General in each country of which she is Head of State. The Governor-General is appointed by her on the advice of ministers in the country concerned and is completely independent of the British government. The Queen maintains direct contact with the Governors-General, but she delegates her constitutional and symbolic powers to them in almost every respect.[4] The Queen's duty is to accept the advice of the Prime Minister in each country. This has provoked controversy in the past. In 1975, the Australian Governor-General, Sir John Kerr, dismissed the Labour Prime Minister Gough Whitlam, and replaced him with Malcolm Fraser, the leader of the National Party. Kerr was widely felt to have acted outside his constitutional powers but the Queen refused demands that she should intervene to dismiss him. Her action considerably strengthened republican sentiment, but the decision was based on her constitutional belief that she was obliged to take the advice of elected ministers in Australia.[5] Similarly, the Queen has regarded the case of Governor-General Peter Hollingworth in 2003 – who, having faced allegations of an earlier rape, was effectively forced to resign – as a matter solely for the Australian government.

The monarchy has not always been divisible in this way. It has effectively evolved from being a single, unified and indivisible Crown into its current position. The indivisible Crown first became untenable in relation to the growing autonomy of the colonial states. The Colonial Laws Validity Act 1865 set out the authority of colonial laws as follows:

'No Colonial Law shall be deemed to have been void or inoperative on the Ground of Repugnancy to the Law of England, unless the same shall be repugnant to the Provisions of some such Act of Parliament, Order, or Regulation as aforesaid.'[6]

In 1926 an Imperial Conference of Commonwealth members adopted the Balfour Formula on the status of the dominions (Canada, New Zealand, the Commonwealth of Australia, the

Union of South Africa, Irish Free State, and Newfoundland). The conference defined the dominions and Britain as:

'...autonomous communities within the British Empire, equal in status, in no way subordinate one to another in any aspect of their domestic or external affairs, though united by a common allegiance to the Crown, and freely associated as members of the British Commonwealth of Nations... Every self-governing member of the Empire is now the master of its destiny. In fact, if not always in form, it is subject to no compulsion whatsoever.'[7]

The British government codified the Balfour Formula's basic principles of equal status and free association in the Statute of Westminster 1931, which has been characterised as the 'Magna Carta of the Commonwealth.' The statute recognised the full legislative autonomy of the dominions and offered all former colonies the right to secede from the Commonwealth. It acknowledged the right of each dominion to control its own domestic and foreign affairs, to establish a diplomatic corps and to be represented at the League of Nations. Each dominion was fully autonomous with equal status, but with common allegiance to the Crown. The British Parliament could no longer legislate for the members of the Commonwealth.

The concept of a divisible monarchy has been developed most clearly in Australia. By 1973 the Australian Parliament was referring to Elizabeth II as Queen of Australia, suggesting that the Crown was divided and that Australia had its own, separate monarch. In 1986 the legal independence of the federal Government was finally confirmed when the Australia Act removed the residual powers of the British Government to intervene in the government of Australia or its individual states. The 1986 Act is an Act of Sovereignty and provides that:

'No Act of the Parliament of the United Kingdom passed after the commencement of this Act shall extend, or be deemed to extend, to the Commonwealth, to a State or to a Territory as part of the law of the Commonwealth, of the State or of the Territory.'[8]

In 1999 a legal case, Sue vs Hill, cemented the issue. The case concerned the requirement that candidates for the Australian Senate could not hold allegiance to a foreign power. In 1999 a certain Heather Hill, holding dual UK and Australian citizenship, stood for the senate. The court therefore sought to establish whether or not the UK, despite its shared Queen, counted as a foreign power. The court found that it did: no exercises of British sovereignty had any legal consequences for Australia. The two nations' heads of state might happen to be the same person, but in constitutional terms they were quite separate.

Reform of the rules of succession

We have recommended changes to the rules of succession of the British monarch. The Statute of Westminster of 1931 is sometimes taken to mean that the UK Parliament cannot alter these rules without the permission of every other Commonwealth country. The constitutional expert Vernon Bogdanor, for example, has suggested that the hurried consultation among the dominions about the abdication in 1936 has given rise to the convention that any change to the rules of succession would require the agreement of every Commonwealth country.[9]

This argument, however, is unconvincing. It ignores the divisibility of the Crown in those states where the Queen is Head of State, as well as various amendments to the constitutions of these independent countries. Other experts argue that consultation with the Commonwealth – most particularly, with those countries of which Elizabeth II is also Queen – would be a matter of courtesy rather than necessity.[10] In the view of Peter Harry of the Commonwealth Institute:

'It is highly debatable whether the members of the Commonwealth would need to ratify any alterations or reforms of the British monarchy. When there was a referendum on the monarchy in Australia in November 1999 the Queen stated that it was a matter entirely for the Australians and kept out of the debate completely. Likewise Britons would be entitled to expect the Commonwealth nations to refrain from interfering with British reforms of the monarchy. It is worth mentioning that the Commonwealth is a voluntary association of independent nations not bound by legal treaties of any kind, which makes it unnecessary for the members to ratify any changes. It would also be incredibly difficult if it were the case. The constitutions of Australia and New Zealand for instance can only be changed through national referen-

dums resulting in a majority of voters in a majority of states voting for the changes.'[11]

The divisibility of the Crown therefore means that there is no constitutional bar on the UK, or indeed any of the other countries of which the Queen is Head of State, changing its rules of succession if it wishes to do so. This should clearly be done through consultation, but no other country can exercise a veto on a constitutional change proposed by the UK for itself. It is inconceivable that the UK would interfere in the right of sovereign states to choose their own Head of State, including those countries who currently have the Queen in that office. But equally the UK could not allow other states to prevent reform of its Head of State simply because they currently share the same incumbent. It is possible, therefore, that if Britain chose to change its rules of succession, say concerning gender preference, but other countries did not, the situation could arise where the monarch of the UK was a different person from the monarch of other Commonwealth countries. There could be a British Queen, but, say, a King of Belize – or, indeed, the reverse. This is the consequence of a divisible monarchy.

In practice this is unlikely to happen. With due consultation we believe it would not be difficult to obtain agreement among Commonwealth countries which retain the Queen as their Head of State on the kinds of reform proposed in this report. It looks very doubtful that any modern state would object to changes to the rules of succession removing discrimination on grounds of gender or religious affiliation. In this sense we do not believe that the position of the Queen as Head of State of other countries presents an obstacle to reforming the monarchy in the UK.

Notes

1   The Commonwealth Secretariat website
    www.thecommonwealth.org
2   Richard Bourne, Head of the Commonwealth Policy Studies Unit,
    London University in written evidence to the Commission
3   *ibid.*

4   From the website www.royal.gov.uk

5   *The Oxford Illustrated History of the British Monarchy*, John Cannon and Ralph Griffiths, OUP 1998

6   Here the term 'colony' is defined in the Act as follows: 'The Term "Colony" shall in this Act include all of Her Majesty's Possessions abroad in which there shall exist a legislature as hereinafter defined except the Channel Islands, the Isle of Man and such Territories as may for the Time being be vested in Her Majesty under or by virtue of any Act of Parliament for the Government of India.'

7   Report of the Inter-Imperial Relations Committee of the Imperial Conference 1926, National Archives of Australia (NAA), NAA: A4640/32

8   Australia Act, 1986

9   *The Monarchy and the Constitution*, Vernon Bogdanor, OUP 1997

10 John Williams, in oral evidence presented to the Commission on 27th November 2002

11 From written evidence to the Commission from Peter Harry of the Commonwealth Institute

Chapter 7

The Royal Family and Household

The focus of this report is on the position of Head of State. But it is impossible to avoid consideration of the wider institution of the monarchy. Indeed, for most of the public the constitutional office is almost certainly of less significance than that wider institution – for them, the monarchy is the royal family and its court, not simply the Head of State.

This is unsurprising. The nature of the institution means that it is difficult to separate the public, official functions from its personal, familial basis. The monarchy is a set of family relationships, stretching into the past, around which the current state apparatus has been built. For much of its history there has been no distinction between the personal right of the monarch and the power of the office. Only as Britain developed into a constitutional, democratic state did such a separation emerge.

Yet the institution that has grown up around the monarch retains many characteristics that are highly personal. The fact that the administrative structure of the institution is known as the Royal Household reflects its private, domestic origins. Behind the symbolism the reality of the structure has changed with the times; but, as we discuss in this chapter, there is still considerable opportunity for further professionalisation of the 'civil service' of the British monarchy.

Similarly, the public role of the extended family blurs the distinction between the personal and the official. The characterisation of the monarchy as a 'family firm' is apt. It is legitimate to question how far this curious blend of informal relations, voluntarism and public office is appropriate within a modern democracy.

Who are the 'royal family'?

Constitutional monarchies obviously differ from presidencies in that the successor to the present incumbent is known some time in advance; but the existence of a wider pool of family members with a public role is also a distinguishing feature. While the spouse of a president may take on some public duties, in no cases do their siblings, nieces and nephews, as is the case with the British Head of State.

The current arrangements for determining the extent and composition of the royal family are based on the George V Settlement of 1917, under which its members are agreed by the monarch in consultation with the Prime Minister. There are no external criteria. It should be stressed at this point that we are here concerned only with the official 'Royal Family' which receives public funds and performs public duties. There are other members of the biological family not included in the 'official' family, a further distinction which must be drawn between the private and the public.

The Royal Family

HM The Queen
HRH Prince Philip, Duke of Edinburgh
HRH The Prince of Wales, and his sons Princes William and Henry
HRH Duke of York and his daughters Beatrice and Eugenie of York
TRH The Earl and Countess of Wessex
HRH The Princess Royal, and her children Peter and Zara Phillips
HRH Princess Alice, Duchess of Gloucester
TRH The Duke and Duchess of Gloucester
TRH The Duke and Duchess of Kent and their children George, Helen and Nicholas
TRH Prince and Princess Michael of Kent and their children Frederick and Gabriella
HRH Princess Alexandra

The current royal family comprises 26 members, who are all to some degree in receipt of public funds. All except the Queen and the Prince of Wales receive parliamentary annuities. However these are almost entirely repaid by the Queen from the monies she receives from the so-called Civil List, also voted by Parliament. Only the Duke of Edinburgh receives a parliamentary annuity which is not repaid by the Queen.

As with the Civil List itself, most of the sums received in parliamentary annuities are spent on staff who support the public duties of family members. As the figures below show, there is some variation in the amounts provided. In all, these parliamentary annuities total just under £1.7 million, which represents the direct cost of maintaining the extended royal family in public office.

Parliamentary Annuities paid to the Royal Family 1990-2010[1]

Duke of Edinburgh	£359,000
Duke of York	£249,000
Earl of Wessex	£141,000
Princess Royal	£228,000
Princess Alice	£87,000
Duke and Duchess of Gloucester	£175,000*
Duke and Duchess of Kent	£236,000*
Princess Alexandra	£225,000*

* These annuities are paid by parliament as a lump sum of £636,000 which is then divided between the Duke and Duchess of Gloucester, the Duke and Duchess of Kent and Princess Alexandra

Roles and duties

While the role of the monarch is fairly well defined, the role of the wider royal family is undoubtedly mutable, shifting with public expectations. The model of the royal family forged in the twentieth century was based on notions of duty and service. Typically, this has involved military service, with most members holding rank or honorary positions within the services. In addition, members of the royal family have served as patrons to hundreds of charitable, cultural and sporting organisations. Prince Philip is patron or president of over 800 organisations; Prince Charles of over 300 organisations, including the Prince's Trust; the Duke of York is patron of, or associated with, more than 100 organisations.

Central to the idea of the public duties of the royal family are the public engagements they undertake, either on state business or as part of their charitable work. Table 7 summarises the number and type of official engagements of each member of the royal family during 2002. It is clear that there is enormous variation in the number performed, with some members very active indeed and others considerably less so (though some caution is needed in interpreting these figures, as engagements vary markedly in the level of commitment they involve).

Some of these public engagements involve members of the royal family deputising for the monarch. This includes relatively minor royals. Both the Duke of Gloucester and Prince Michael of Kent, for example, have represented the Queen overseas at royal coronations and weddings, state funerals and independence celebrations.

In some ways the evolution of these charitable and state duties can be seen as an adaptation to the changing nature of British society during the twentieth century, where an extended Royal Family needed to find a role. Whereas presidencies fulfil their ceremonial and constitutional functions with just an individual and occasionally a spouse, the British monarchy found in the idea of 'good works' a justification for retaining this wide circle of public figures.

It is easy to see why the public duties performed by members of the royal family in this way are seen as extremely valuable. Royalty provides what has been described as a kind of 'magic dust', attracting public attention and creating a sense of occasion when public appearances are made. Members of the royal family have been strongly appreciated by those charities and organisations with which they are associated, investing the charity with a particular kind of value and allowing it to attach special

Table 7: Royal Engagements 2002 [2]

	A	B	C	D	E
The Queen	229	86	156	471	74
Duke of Edinburgh	279	168	40	487	91
Prince of Wales	215	97	165	477	84
Duke of York	133	51	17	201	304
Earl of Wessex	170	57	30	257	142
Countess of Wessex	181	48	11	240	87
Princess Royal	268	89	53	410	159
Duke of Gloucester	113	48	41	202	29
Duchess of Gloucester	95	20	11	126	29
Duke of Kent	135	43	12	190	41
Princess Alexandra	83	29	24	136	24

A	Official visits, opening ceremonies and other engagements
B	Receptions, lunches, dinners and banquets
C	Other engagements including investitures, meetings and audiences given
D	Total number of engagements in the UK
E	Total number of engagements on official overseas tours

significance to events. In the USA it is notable that this role is generally filled by celebrities. The 'public' nature of royal patronage takes the role out of the private realm, attaching shared values to the endorsement. In this sense one could almost describe the monarchy as a 'public sector' version of the private celebrity industry. It represents the values of public duty rather than merely of an individual.

In addition to their public duties, some members of the royal family also pursue private interests, including commercial concerns. Such activities have caused public concern on occasions, notably in 2001 when certain of the public relations business activities of Sophie of Wessex were uncovered by a newspaper, and Edward was criticised for the behaviour of his film company in making a commercial film about Prince William. There is at present no bar to publicly-supported family members undertaking such commercial activities; the only constraint appears to be a kind of self-regulation by the family, usually in the form of advice from Buckingham Palace. But this usually appears to come in response to problems, when damage has already been caused, rather than to prevent it.

A new settlement

It is unusual for as many public roles to be associated with the Head of State as is the case with the British royal family, even in other European constitutional monarchies. Most limit the public roles and their remuneration to the Head of State and the heir. Constitutionally there is little reason for retaining the public role of an extended royal family at all. But while the current system is perhaps not one that would be designed from scratch, it is nevertheless the system we have, and it has developed a number of advantages, not least in terms of the value of the philanthropic work performed.

Nevertheless, there has been a perception in some quarters that there are too many peripheral members of the royal family receiving public funding. In general it is not the number of royals in principle which seems to matter – nor even the amount of money they receive – but the duties they carry out. The objections relate to those members of the family who carry out very few public duties or who combine them with apparently conflicting commercial activities.

Our own conclusion is that the number of official members of the royal family receiving public funds should be reduced. More importantly, the status of being an active member of the royal family – and consequently eligible for state remuneration – should be linked to the duties performed. Determining the optimal size of the family is not a straightforward task. But the George V settlement, allowing the monarch to define who is a member of the family in discussion with the Prime Minister, should be ended. Instead, we believe that the royal family should be limited to the monarch, the monarch's spouse, their offspring, and the children of the heir. Once a person is identified as a working member of the royal family, he or she should then be able to continue regardless of changes in family relationships such as the death of the monarch. However on the maturing of the 'next generation' older members should also be allowed to withdraw from public life if they so wish. This reform should affect only new additions to the royal family, so that current members are not stripped of their position without their consent.

At the same time, we believe that members of the royal family who do not wish to have a public role should be able to 'opt out' of a job for which they may have little inclination or aptitude. The mere fact of family relationships should not force any individual into taking a public role which they do not want. But those who do decide to stay in the royal family should realise that it is a job, a public appointment, and one to be taken seriously. If a member of the royal family chooses to receive Civil List payment they must carry out public duties and behave accordingly. We do not believe that these duties are compatible with commercial activities. Family members should either be in or out of public life. Those who opt out of public life would lose public financial support. They would become private citizens, free to live and work as they chose, with appropriate protection if necessary. Having opted out of public life, members of the royal family would not be allowed to 'opt back in' again.

Public expectations of the kinds of public duties which members of the royal family should undertake inevitably change over time, though the expectation of charitable work has been fairly constant. We do not believe that the content of public duties can be formally specified. Given that there is no choice of selection, flexibility needs to be retained to allow jobs to be matched to different individuals' skills and interests. But it is important that the public engagements and roles should be chosen to be representative of the nation as a whole. We have already argued the importance of the principle of 'representativeness' if the monarchy is to continue to be seen as relevant to a changing society. It is in the public duties that this principle can most easily be made manifest. The royal family needs explicitly to associate itself with all parts of Britain: with its four nations and different regions, its diversity of ethnic groups, with all age groups, social structures, cultural, sporting and leisure activities, employment patterns and so on. In this way the institution can more closely reflect – and be seen to reflect – the modern nation it serves.

The Royal Household

The Royal Household is effectively the civil service department for the Head of State, providing a secretariat function for the public duties of the monarch and royal family. But it is also the private household of the family, incorporating domestic staff. As in other aspects of the monarchy's affairs, the distinction between the public and private aspects of the institution of Head of State is blurred.

Of course the present structure originated in an entirely different context, with the monarch occupying a more personally powerful and political position. In the 17th and 18th centuries the Royal Household was much more politicised; with each change of government staff were sacked and re-appointed and the Household was much more integrated with the state apparatus.

As the organisation has evolved it has adapted itself to new circumstances. Yet there remain good grounds for a thorough review in order to address some of the failings that have become apparent in recent years. Problems have included the quality of management, the availability of good advice, questions of recruitment and staffing, tensions (or at least a lack of co-ordination) between Buckingham and St James's Palaces, and the lack of clarity in the distinction between the public role and private lives of members of the royal family.

Composition and role

The Royal Household consists of the Queen's Household plus the Households of other members of the Royal Family who undertake public engagements, in particular the Prince of Wales. It employs some 645 full-time staff. Most are based in Buckingham Palace although there are also offices in St James's Palace, Windsor Castle and the Royal Mews. In addition to the full-time members of staff, the Household includes the so-called 'Great Officers of State' who take part in important royal ceremonies, and ladies-in-waiting, who are appointed personally by the Queen and other female members of the royal family.

This organisation provides administrative support for the monarchy including a 'civil service' role in its public duties, as well as being the private staff of family members, from secretaries to servants. The Household is under the overall authority of the Lord Chamberlain. His role is to oversee its conduct and general business including close involvement with all senior appointments. He is also the channel of communication between the sovereign and the House of Lords. Until 1924 the Lord Chamberlain was a political appointment. It is no longer, though the current incumbent, Lord Luce, happens to be a former Conservative politician.

The Royal Household is divided into five departments:

The Private Secretary's Office
The present position of Private Secretary dates from the late 19th century, although George III and his two successors also had Private Secretaries for particular reasons. His primary role today is as political adviser to the monarch. He is the channel of communication between the Head of State and the government, in the UK and in the fifteen other countries of which she is also Queen. The post is a personal appointment made by the Queen, rather than a political one, although the Prime Minister and Cabinet Secretary, with whom much of his work is done, are consulted. As Vernon Bogdanor explains:

'The Private Secretary and his assistants are the only people who are solely concerned with the interests of the Sovereign. The interests of the ministers are necessarily different, since they may, unwittingly, make requests of the Sovereign which would create awkward precedents for the future. Only the Private Secretary can protect the Sovereign from the embarrassment of granting such requests. Moreover, a Private Secretary may have to suggest to the Sovereign that he should exercise prerogatives in a way that the Government might not like; he might, for example, have to suggest that the Sovereign should refuse a dissolution. Therefore he cannot be a Government appointee.'[3]

The Office also has an important co-ordinating role within the Household, liaising with the Households of other members of the royal family. The Co-ordination and Research Unit (CRU) within the Private Secretary's Office researches and plans the programmes of members of the royal family. This includes ensuring that invitations are given due consideration, as well as planning special 'theme days' for the Queen and ensuring that full geographic coverage of the UK is achieved in engagements. The CRU played an important role in developing the Golden Jubilee programme in 2002.

The Privy Purse and Treasurer's Office
The Keeper of the Privy Purse is responsible for the management of the Queen's financial affairs, including the management of the revenues from the Duchy of Lancaster and the Civil List. He also oversees the Grants-in-Aid from government departments for the maintenance of the Occupied Royal Palaces and for royal travel and for personnel matters in the Royal Household. The department is also responsible for the Queen's private estates and for the commercial activities of the Royal Collection Trust. (These are all discussed further in the next chapter.)

The Master of the Household's Department
The Master of the Household is responsible for domestic arrangements and staff, as well as the catering and official entertaining at Buckingham Palace and other royal residences. It is the largest department in the Royal Household with a staff of around 280. These include cleaners, porters, specialist furniture craftsmen, pages and footmen. The position of Master of the Household was first created by the Household reforms of 1539. Originally there were four Masters but by the late 17th century this number had been reduced to one and the post became a sinecure. Under Prince Albert's reorganisation of the Household in the 1840s the Master was put in charge of the entire domestic establishment.

The Lord Chamberlain's Office

Despite its name, this department is as independent of the Lord Chamberlain as the other departments. Formerly best known by reason of the Lord Chamberlain's function of censoring the theatre (a role originating in medieval times and abolished in 1968), the department concentrates on the administration of inward state visits by overseas heads of state, investitures, garden parties, the State Opening of Parliament, Garter ceremonial and royal weddings and funerals. It also acts as a link between the monarch and the Diplomatic Heads of Mission based in the UK, and co-ordinates all matters relating to honours.

The Royal Collection Department

The duties of the Royal Collection Department are the cataloguing, conservation, cleaning, restoration and display of the pictures, sculptures and other works of art collected by British monarchs over the centuries, and now held by the Queen in trust for her successors and for the nation. The department is also responsible for making the Collection accessible to the public, either by display in the state apartments of palaces open to the public, and in the Queen's Gallery, or by loans to exhibitions. The activities of the Royal Collection Department are funded by the Royal Collection Trust. The Trust's income is generated by its trading subsidiary, Royal Collection Enterprises Limited, which is responsible for managing access by the public to Windsor Castle, Buckingham Palace and the Palace of Holyrood House. The company is also responsible for the management of the images and intellectual property rights to the Royal Collection. (This is further discussed in the next chapter.)

Occasional, part-time members of the Queen's Household include the Great Officers of State (such as the Lord Great Chamberlain and the Earl Marshal) and others such as the Lord Steward and the Master of the Horse (titular heads of the Master of the Household's Department and of the Royal Mews). These members are unpaid, and play a ceremonial role, having little to do with the daily running of the Royal Household.

The Ladies-in-waiting are appointed personally by the Queen and other female members of the royal family to accompany them on public engagements, including national occasions and state visits abroad. They often handle the flowers, cards and presents which the Queen and other members of the royal family receive during their visits and walkabouts. They also deal with the Queen's private correspondence and reply to letters from the public, especially those from children. Equerries support the Queen in her official duties and private life, as members of a small team responsible for the detailed planning and execution of the Queen's daily programme. Equerries are seconded from the armed forces for three years.

An Office of the Head of State

The structure of the Royal Household is, in many respects, archaic. But there are more substantive concerns about its ability to meet the needs of a modern institution of Head of State. In particular we believe that there needs to be stronger, more co-ordinated and professional management. This is not to criticise those who currently work within the Household. However, the merging of the administration of the public and private affairs of the Head of State, along with other specific problems which arise from the particular characteristics of our hereditary system, create difficulties which we believe need to be addressed.

The first of these is the lack of management co-ordination which stems from the system of two palaces, Buckingham and St James's. The CRU located in the Private Secretary's Office has been useful as a co-ordinating mechanism, most recently in planning the Golden Jubilee celebrations. But problems remain, notably in the existence of two, sometimes seemingly rival, press and communications offices. We note that Lord Luce, the Lord Chamberlain, has expressed the hope of greater co-ordination between the two courts through the establishment of a unified press office.[4] We believe that this reform is overdue.

In some ways achieving greater coherence between the palace offices is not entirely straightforward because a known successor to the Head of State can be 'in waiting' for a number of years. The hereditary system can inevitably lead to tensions, and it is probably not possible to stop the heir appointing his or her own separate advisors. But the administrative system should be designed to prevent such tensions emerging whenever possible and to co-ordinate the institution and family as a whole.

To achieve this co-ordination we believe an externally recruited professional Chief Executive should be appointed to Buckingham Palace to manage the public affairs of the royal family. It would be sensible if the Royal Household itself were re-titled the Office of the Head of State to mark a clear distinction between the public institution and the private affairs of its members. The Chief Executive should be the equivalent of a departmental Permanent Secretary in the civil service. Although located in Buckingham Palace, this post should have overall responsibility for the public duties of the royal family as a whole, and specifically for co-ordinating Buckingham and St James's Palaces. The Chief Executive should be the senior management position in the Royal Household or Office of the Head of State, working directly for the monarch and able to give orders to all other palace staff with the Queen's authority. The appointment should be openly advertised and made by the monarch on the advice of the Public Appointments Commission.

The administration, staffing and financing of the private and domestic functions of the Royal Household should be completely separated from its public elements.

Recruitment and employment

In addition to a Chief Executive, the Royal Household or Office of Head of State needs properly constituted recruitment and staffing procedures for senior posts that relate to the public duties of the Head of State. Within Buckingham Palace virtually all posts relating to public duties are properly advertised but this does not appear to be the case throughout the Royal Household. As a public institution, the staff of the Office of the Head of State should be civil servants with the same status as those of other state departments, and the recruitment procedures should be the same. As well as leading to greater professionalism, opening up the recruitment processes of the present Royal Household should lead to greater diversity within the staff, going some way to improve the representativeness of the institution.

In addition to proper recruitment procedures, within some parts of the current Royal Household there is evidently a need for much greater managerial professionalism. This has been acknowledged in the Peat Report of 2003, which investigated the rape allegation made by an employee in the Household of the Prince of Wales.[5] Although the report found no evidence that there was an 'improper cover-up' of the case, it raised a number of issues regarding the professionalism with which the allegation was dealt with and the way in which personnel matters as a whole are handled by St James's Palace. The report found that the case was not properly investigated, partly because the allegation was not believed and partly because it came to light during the handover from one Private Secretary to another. The matter was delegated to a relatively junior personnel officer. The report found the complainant's personnel file to be incomplete and deficient and there were no clear guidelines on how such records should be kept or such matters handled. Additionally, in the light of its evidence on the improper handling of gifts made to members of the royal family (which we discuss in the next chapter), the Peat Report acknowledged the importance of public institutions having proper professional management.

Advice

Along with reforming the management and recruitment of the Royal Household itself, we believe that the royal family would benefit from the appointment of an independent body of advisors. The Head of State is an important public office and as such it should be guided by advice from a range of sources on how the activities of the monarch and the royal family can best serve the public and the country. Advisors can help in particular to ensure that the institution is, and looks, as representative as possible of the diversity of modern Britain. The advisors themselves, publicly known and appointed, could help to do this. As other countries have found, a Head of State seen to be reaching out to and soliciting opinions and advice from all sections of society gains particular respect.

Notes

1 These are currently fixed every ten years. The 1990 settlement has been extended without alteration until 2010

2 This table is provided by Mr Tim O'Donovan in a letter to *The Times* on 1st January 2003, based on reports in the Court Circular

3 *The Monarchy and the Constitution,* Vernon Bogdanor, OUP 1995

4 'Palaces seek truce on press infighting', Matt Wells, The *Guardian*, 25th January 2002

5 *Report to His Royal Highness The Prince of Wales* by Sir Michael Peat and Edmund Lawson QC, March 2003

Chapter 8

Finance, Property and Taxation

The Queen is often described as 'one of the world's richest women'.[1] Certainly she and her family hold considerable wealth, accumulated over several centuries. But discussion of the wealth of the royal family is frequently confused by a failure to distinguish between those assets which belong privately to the Windsor family and those which are associated with the monarch as Head of State, and which should therefore properly be described as belonging to the public. These include some of the most magnificent buildings in Britain and some of the finest art in the world. This confusion is perhaps an unsurprising consequence of a hereditary system in which the private family and the public institution have been intertwined.

In addition to the sovereign's public wealth she receives considerable revenue funding from the state in order to fulfil her public duties. Yet the way in which the office of Head of State is financed is complex and opaque, the product of the institution's long history and gradual evolution. Again there is confusion between public and private income.

In this final chapter we consider how the office of Head of State should be financed in a modern democracy, and how the various properties and assets that have accrued to the monarchy over the centuries should be dealt with in future. The key principles underpinning our approach are transparency – particularly over finance – and the clear separation of the public and private. These are essential if the monarchy is to be seen to serve the needs of the country today.

Table 8: Head of State Expenditure met from Public Funds
(www.royal.gov.uk)

Year to 31 March	2002-03 £ 000	2001-02 £ 000
The Queen's Civil List (figures are for calendar years 2002 and 2001)	9,759	8,153
Notional pension contributions	43	45
Parliamentary annuities	359	1,000
Grants-in-Aid:		
Property services	16,627	15,522
Communications and information	526	643
Travel by air and rail	4,241	4,936
Expenditure met directly by Government Departments and the Crown Estate:		
HM Treasury – administration of honours	410	432
Ministry of Defence – equerries and orderlies	957	914
Historic Scotland – maintenance of the Palace of Holyrood House	2,253	2,147
Foreign and Commonwealth Office – state visits to and by the Queen and liaison with the Diplomatic Corps	310	575
Department for Culture, Media and Sport – ceremonial occasions	52	312
Crown Estate – maintenance of the Home Park at Windsor Castle	587	592
Other	56	24
Total expenditure	36,180	35,295

Paying for the Head of State

Every country has to pay for its Head of State. As we have already argued, the overall cost of the post is not, we believe, a good basis upon which to argue about the form it should take. The office of the UK Head of State is relatively inexpensive compared with some other European comparators. The official expenditure relating to the Queen's duties as Head of State, which is met from public funds, was £36.2 million for 2002-03 (see Table 8 on previous page). However this excludes certain costs such as security and military expenditure. Others have estimated that the true cost is somewhere between £35 and £60 million per year.[2] Total expenditure has been reduced in recent years. The figure for 2002-3 represents a reduction of 59 per cent since 1991-92.

Funding for the monarchy comes from four main sources:

- The Civil List, voted by Parliament, which meets the expenses of the Royal Household
- Grants-in-Aid, provided by Parliament through government departments, for royal travel, for the upkeep of royal palaces, and for communications and information
- The Privy Purse, funded by revenue from the Duchy of Lancaster, which provides an income for the monarch
- The Duchy of Cornwall, which provides an income for the Prince of Wales.

The Civil List

The Civil List is the best known element of royal funding, although it is not always fully understood. Often thought of as payments to individual members of the royal family, the funding is in fact provided by Parliament to the Queen to meet the official expenses of the Royal Household so that she can fulfil her role as Head of State.

The Civil List dates back to the restoration of the monarchy in 1660, but the current system was created on the accession of George III in 1760. Since 1697 the monarch had received an annual grant from Parliament as a contribution to the Civil List, that is, to the costs of civil government (such as judges' and ambassadors' salaries) and the expenses of the Royal Household. In 1760 it was decided that the whole cost of the Civil List should be provided by Parliament in return for the surrender of the King's 'hereditary revenues', principally the net surplus of the Crown Estate, for the duration of his reign. This arrangement still applies today, although civil government costs are now paid by Parliament rather than financed directly by the monarch from the Civil List. The state continues to receive the net surplus of the Crown Estate, £163m in 2001-02, for the duration of each monarch's reign.

About 70 per cent of Civil List expenditure is used to pay the salaries of staff working directly for the Queen. The funding also meets the costs of functions such as royal garden parties (the Queen entertains over 48,000 people each year) and official entertainment during state visits. Members of the royal family are nominally 'on the Civil List' although they are not paid directly from it. They receive separate Parliamentary Annuities which are then repaid to the Treasury by the Queen from her own income from the Duchy of Lancaster.

In 1990 the Civil List was set by Parliament as a fixed annual amount of £7.9 million for a period of 10 years. The budget for each year's projected net Civil List spending is reviewed by the Treasury, which audits the accounts and verifies that the Household's financial management is in line with best practice. Details of expenditure are published in an annual summary, *Report of the Royal Trustees*, and in a full annual report which was published for the first time in June 2002. The annual summary of Head of State expenditure and reports for the Grants-in-Aid for property services and royal travel are also now published at the same time (these are discussed below).

The Civil List settlement in 1990 allowed for an inflationary increase of 7.8 per cent a year. In fact inflation has been far below this. Consequently a reserve of £37 million has built up. The Civil List Annual Report for 2001 explains that to allow for inflation the 1972 Civil List Act provides for the amount of the Civil List to be higher than estimated expenditure so that annual surpluses can be accumulated to cover deficits in later years or to

carry forward into a subsequent ten year period. If there is surplus carried forward the Royal Trustees will take it into account
when making their recommendation for the annual amount of
the Civil List for the next ten years.

During the ten year period to 31st December 2000, annual
Civil List expenditure reached £6.5m, still short of the annual
amount of £7.9 million set in 1990, and a reserve of £35m was
built up. In view of this, and in order to draw down the reserve,
the annual Civil List amount was left at £7.9m for a further ten
years.

In 2001 Civil List spending at £8.4m exceeded the £7.9m
Treasury allowance. £0.5mwas therefore taken from the reserve
to finance the difference. Nevertheless the 2001 accounts show
that the value of the reserve grew from £35.6m in 2000 to £37.1m.
The investments undertaken by the Royal Household
Investment Committee, which since 1990 has invested the surplus on the Civil List, boosted the Civil List reserve by £2m
despite the fall in stock market values.

The accounts show that Buckingham Palace expects Civil List
spending again to exceed the £7.9m a year Treasury allowance in
2002 – but it expects the interest from the money market deposits
to once again cover the difference. That would have left the
Royal Family with £37m of taxpayers' money in the bank. The
Guardian reported in June 2002 that Buckingham Palace had confirmed that its aim was to keep the equivalent of one year's
spending in the reserve – about £37m – and that none of the
money could be recouped by the Treasury until the Queen died
and a new Civil List was agreed.[3]

Grants-in-Aid

Each year the royal family carries out about 4,000 official
engagements in the UK and overseas. These engagements
involve a significant amount of travel. Such travel needs to meet
presentational, efficiency and security requirements.

Up to March 1997 the costs of official royal travel by air and
rail were met by the Ministry of Defence, the Department for
Transport (DfT) and the Foreign and Commonwealth Office. At
the Royal Household's suggestion, responsibility for the expen-

diture was transferred to the Household with effect from April 1997. The Royal Household now receives annual funding to meet the costs of official royal travel in the form of a royal travel Grant-in-Aid from Parliament, through the DfT.

Table 9:Grant-in-Aid and Expenditure on Royal Travel (www.royal.gov.uk)

Year to 31 March	2003 £ 000	2002 £ 000
Amount of Grant-in-Aid voted by Parliament	5,444	6,010
Air Travel:		
Helicopters	2,064	1,961
Fixed wing (civil operators)	456	1,483
Fixed wing (32 Squadron)	476	459
	2,996	3,903
Rail Travel:		
Royal Train	872	675
Other	31	28
	903	703
Administration and other:		
Sea travel (civil operators)	3	–
Administrator	352	347
Interest	(13)	(17)
	342	330
Total net expenditure	4,241	4,936

The Royal Household's management of the Grant-in-Aid is subject to supervision by the DfT. The Royal Household annually submits a rolling five-year plan to the DfT for approval as well as detailed quarterly reports and a detailed budget at the start of each financial year. To improve accountability and transparency an annual report is published which includes the income and expenditure account.

The majority of royal travel expenditure is spent on the Queen's helicopter and chartered or scheduled fixed-wing aircraft provided by civil operators, used particularly for major overseas state visits. Fixed-wing Royal Air Force aircraft from 32 (The Royal) Squadron and the Royal Train are also used. Official travel by car for the Queen is paid for from the Civil List and for the Duke of Edinburgh from his parliamentary annuity. Official travel by car for other members of the royal family is paid for from private sources. The Grant-in-Aid for the year to 31 March 2003 was £5.4m; actual expenditure was £4.2m. The royal train budget was £0.87m in 2002-03, a reduction by around 60 per cent in absolute terms since the Grant-in-Aid began in 1997.

Table 10:Expenditure on Palaces (www.royal.gov.uk)

Year to 31 March	2003 £ 000	2002 £ 000
Buckingham Palace	6,215	7,525
Buckingham Palace Mews and Gardens	1,636	1,478
St James's Palace	1,754	1,685
Clarence House and Marlborough House Mews	2,355	446
Kensington Palace	489	353
Hampton Court Mews and Paddocks	148	228
Windsor Castle	2,523	2,378
Windsor Castle Royal Mews	560	382
Windsor Home and Great Parks	1,310	1,036
Central Costs	968	861
	17,958	16,372
Visitor contribution	(1331)	(850)
Total net expenditure	16,627	15,522

Through the Department for Culture, Media and Sport (DCMS) Parliament also provides a property maintenance Grant-in-Aid annually to the Royal Household. The money is used to meet the cost of buildings maintenance, and of certain utilities and related services. From April 1991 the Property Section of the Royal Household took over day-to-day management and operating responsibility. As with the Grant-in-Aid for travel, the Royal Household annually submits a rolling five-year plan to the DCMS for its approval as well as detailed quarterly reports and a detailed budget at the start of each financial year. The Grant-in-Aid for 1990-91 was £25.7 million; it was reduced to £16.6 million in 2002-03. In addition a small grant-in-aid is provided for expenditure on communications and information. This amounted to £0.5m in 2003-03.

The Duchy of Lancaster and the Privy Purse

The Duchy of Lancaster is a landed estate of approximately 19,268 hectares held in trust for the monarch since 1399. The surplus from the Duchy of Lancaster finances the Privy Purse, which for the year to 31 March 2003 amounted to £7.31 million before tax. While the income of the Duchy is essentially the private income of the sovereign, the capital assets themselves do not belong to her and are not hers to dispose of. The Duchy may sell assets from time to time but the policy is to apply any proceeds to maintain its capital base for the future. Moreover the current Queen uses much of the revenue from the Duchy to meet official expenses incurred by other members of the royal family. For example, the Queen uses around £1.5m to cover the official expenses of Princess Anne, Prince Andrew, Prince Edward and a handful of minor royals, and to pay the wages of those members of the royal retinue whose salaries are not covered by Civil List money.

Constitutionally the Duchy of Lancaster is the responsibility of the Chancellor of the Duchy of Lancaster, who is now normally a Cabinet Minister and is accountable to Parliament for the running of the Duchy. It is formally the Chancellor of the Duchy of Lancaster who has the final say each year on how much is paid from the Duchy to the Privy Purse to meet royal expenses.

A Treasury historical note implies that the Duchy of Lancaster was largely overlooked during the handover from monarch to state in 1760 because it 'only produced the derisory sum of £16 18s 4d in that year.'[4] In 1971 the Government allowed the continuation of the existing arrangements because revenue from the Duchy of Lancaster (then worth £300,000 a year) was being used to fund the deficit in the Civil List caused by inflation. As the Treasury files show: 'It may not be easy to offer a convincing defence for the retention of so large a sum were it not for the fact that the Privy Purse is meeting the deficit on the Civil List in 1970 and 1971.'[5] With the current healthy state of the royal finances, this defence no longer seems convincing.

For much of the Queen's reign the revenues of the estate have not only consisted of rents and dividends from the Duchy's land and £72m investment portfolio (all of which are exempt from Capital Gains Tax and Corporation Tax); the estate has also benefited from the Duchy's so-called *bona vacantia*. These are the proceeds from the sale of land in Merseyside and Yorkshire, and from the rest of the Duchy, where people have died intestate with no traceable next of kin. Over the years the sale of this land has often made up more than 30 per cent of the Duchy's revenue. In 2000 more than £2.1m was raised from 276 people who died intestate and the proceeds of 232 companies which were dissolved. Since 1993 the money from this source has gone into a Duchy of Lancaster benevolent fund.

The Duchy of Cornwall

The Duchy of Cornwall was created in 1337 by a charter ruling that each future Duke of Cornwall would be the eldest surviving son of the monarch – and the heir to the throne. The Duchy's main purpose has been to provide an independent income for the heir apparent. That income covers the cost of both the public and private life of the current Duke, the Prince of Wales. Neither he nor his sons receives an annuity from Parliament.

Prince Charles became the 24th Duke of Cornwall on the Queen's accession in 1952. He is in effect a trustee, and is not entitled to the proceeds of disposals of assets. The Prince must pass on the estate intact so that it continues to provide an income from its assets for future Dukes of Cornwall. When there is no male heir, the title to the Duchy reverts to the monarch and its income to the Exchequer. This procedure was followed when Elizabeth II was heir.

The Duchy's net surplus for the year to 31st March 2003 was £9.9m. The Prince's annual expenditure on public activities in 2003-03 was £8.7m. In addition to the income from the Duchy of Cornwall, this was financed by grants-in-aid (£2.8m) and government departments (£0.3m). His personal expenditure and tax contribution amounted to £4.2m, leaving a surplus of £0.08m. Detailed records are kept to determine the split between public and private expenditure.[6]

As there is an ongoing programme of development and renovation across the Duchy, much of the money made by the Duchy is ploughed back into it, for example by the building of new properties for retired tenants. In addition, the Duke of Cornwall's Benevolent Fund makes significant donations each year to charitable organisations (such as those working on environmental issues) in Cornwall and the South West.

A new settlement

The current arrangements for revenue funding of the Head of State and for the wider institution of the royal family are complicated and anomalous. As Vernon Bogdanor has put it:

'there are probably few members of the public who understand either the arrangements or their rationale.'[7]

These complications derive from the historic development of the monarchy as Head of State, notably from the unity of office and individual. While this is more significant in the case of property – the subject of the next section – it is also true of revenue funding. The present arrangements confuse the private income of the royal family with the state income which one would expect to find provided for the Head of State in a modern nation. We believe that reform is needed to bring proper clarity and accountability to the way the office of Head of State is financed.

First, the royal finances need to be more transparent. The current opacity of the sources of royal income and detail of expenditure leads to public misunderstanding and should not be acceptable in a democracy. Currently the Civil List Act 1972 requires the Royal Trustees to report to Parliament on the royal finances at least once every ten years. This reflected the view of the 1971 Select Committee that ten yearly rather than annual reports were more consistent with the honour and dignity of the monarch. The last Royal Trustees' report to be laid before Parliament was in July 2000. More recently annual reports have been published by Buckingham Palace and, from 2003, St James's Palace. However, these are for information only; they are not required to be laid before Parliament and remain less than wholly transparent. We recommend that annual public reports be presented to Parliament, in a comprehensive and readily understandable form.

Second, the way in which the office of Head of State and the wider royal family is paid for needs to be substantially reformed. There are indications that the case for change has been considered by the Palaces in the past. In the late 1980s Prince Charles suggested reversing the 1760 arrangements by which the sovereign transferred hereditary revenues, including the income from the Crown Estates, to the government in exchange for the Civil List. The Civil List and all departmental expenditure for the monarchy would be abandoned, with the income from the Crown Estates reverting from the Treasury to the sovereign. As Vernon Bogdanor puts it:

> '...by strengthening royal control over finance, [this] would make the monarchy more autonomous and therefore more effective, and also remove contentious items such as the Civil List from the political agenda... it would avoid the misunderstanding by which increases in the Civil List were seen as 'pay rises for the Queen.'[8]

However, we reject this proposal. The public position of Head of State requires formal and accountable public funding. The greater autonomy that Bogdanor anticipates from such a solution would simply further blur the distinction between the private income of the monarch and the public funding of the office of Head of State. Instead we believe that all aspects of finance for the royal family should be combined into a single payment, subject to a vote in Parliament. This would mean combining the current Civil List with the Privy Purse, the Grants-in-Aid and, with respect to the Prince of Wales, the income from the Duchy of Cornwall, into a single, secure and accountable public revenue stream for the office of Head of State and the working royal family. This should cover both the salaries of working members of the family and all the expenses associated with their public duties.

Switching to a single payment would mean that the entire budget for the royal family would be dependent on an annual vote in Parliament. This might be felt to subject the budget to political pressures, but this would be no more than decisions made by Parliament on the financing of other essential departments of state. Some of these pressures could be lessened by instituting a ten year settlement as is currently the case with the Civil List.

At the same time we believe that the title to the Duchies of Lancaster and Cornwall, and to the Crown Estate, should be transferred formally to the nation. They should be managed by the Crown Estates Commissioners, appointed by the government. The state would not be allowed to sell this land; it should be held in trust for the nation, as with other national heritage sites.

These reforms would have the effect of establishing a clear separation of private and public income. They would ensure that the public office of Head of State was properly financed by the taxpayer, as in other countries, under normal conditions of public accountability.

Property and wealth

In addition to its revenue funding, the British monarchy holds a range of properties and other assets. These comprise land and buildings, the Royal Collection of jewels, art and other artefacts, and financial wealth. Some of these assets are entirely privately owned by the sovereign and her family, others are wholly public. Some, as in the Duchies of Lancaster and Cornwall already discussed, are notionally public but the titles are in fact held in trust by the monarch and family.

The Crown Estate and personal properties

Much of the land and property – although not the two Duchies, which operate under their own statutes – comprises the Crown Estate. The Crown Estate incorporates an urban estate including significant London holdings, particularly in Regent Street, Regent's Park and St James's, as well as almost 120,000 hectares of agricultural land and extensive marine assets throughout the UK.

The Crown Estate is part of the hereditary possessions of the reigning monarch, although it is not private property – it is inherited with the title. Between 1066 and 1760 the land was the property of the monarch, who was able to do whatever he or she pleased with it. In 1760, an agreement was reached with Parliament that, although the property would remain in the monarch's name, all net revenue from the estates would be given to Parliament each year in return for the Civil List. The property cannot be sold and is held in trust by the Queen and her heirs. The profits of the Crown Estate in the year ending 31st March 2003 were £163.3 million.[9]

The Crown Estate is run by the Crown Estate Commissioners and their staff. There are seven Commissioners, appointed by the Queen. Only the Chief Executive is full-time; the others, including the Chairman, are part-time. The First Commissioner has an audience with the Queen once a year to present an annual report.

The most visible royal properties are the palaces, owned either by the Crown or the Queen. These properties fall into three categories: the royal palaces which are occupied by the monarch, other members of the royal family and their staff; the unoccupied palaces which serve primarily as museums; and those properties which are the personal property of the royal family.

Occupied Royal Palaces

The occupied palaces are Crown property, rather than the Queen's personal property. Held in trust for future generations, their maintenance and upkeep is one the expenses met by the government in return for the sovereign's surrender of the hereditary revenue from the Crown Estate. They are administered by the Royal Household. Approximately 1,000 people work at the occupied royal palaces. The Queen invites approximately 70,000 guests annually to the palaces and there are approximately 1.5 million paying visitors. The main properties in this category are:

- Buckingham Palace (including the Queen's Gallery)
- St James's Palace
- Clarence House
- Marlborough Mews House
- Residential and office areas of Kensington Palace
- Windsor Castle and buildings in the Home and Great Parks at Windsor
- Hampton Court Mews and Paddocks
- The Palace of Holyroodhouse

In addition this category includes 269 properties available for residential use on a rental basis, mainly by staff and pensioners; and twelve properties used as communal residential accommodation for staff.

Historic Royal Palaces

As with the occupied royal palaces, these properties are not owned by the sovereign; they are held by her as monarch rather than as an individual, and must be passed on to her successor. The Secretary of State for Culture, Media and Sport contracts their management to Historic Royal Palaces, which is responsible for their care, conservation and presentation to the public. Historic Royal Palaces is a charity and receives no Grant-in-Aid, relying instead on the revenues generated by the palaces to meet the costs of maintaining and managing them. The Trust publishes an annual report which includes its financial accounts. The palaces are:

- The Tower of London
- Hampton Court Palace
- Kensington Palace State Apartments and Royal Ceremonial Dress Collection
- The Banqueting House, Whitehall

- Kew Palace with Queen Charlotte's Cottage
- Brighton Pavilion
- Osborne House

The Palace of Westminster falls into a slightly different category. Control of the Houses of Parliament was originally vested in the Lord Great Chamberlain as the Queen's representative. In 1965, however, control passed jointly to the Speaker, for the House of Commons part of the building, and to the Lord Chancellor, for the House of Lords' part. The Lord Great Chamberlain retains joint responsibility with the Speaker and the Lord Chancellor for the Crypt, Chapel and Westminster Hall. Since 1992, the Parliamentary Estate has been cared for and maintained by the Parliamentary Works Directorate of the Serjeant at Arms Department. The title to the outbuilding was transferred from the Department of the Environment following the passage of the Parliamentary Corporate Bodies Act 1992.

Private estates

Balmoral Castle and Sandringham House are the personal property of the Queen, rather than royal palaces belonging to the Crown. These estates are privately owned and can be sold or bequeathed as the Queen wishes.

The Sunninghill Park estate was purchased by the Crown Estate Commissioners in 1945. However, a walled garden of around five acres was purchased on behalf of the Queen from the Commissioners in 1988 and a two-storey red brick house was completed in 1990, as a home for the Duke and Duchess of York and their family.

Highgrove has been the private residence of the Prince of Wales since 1980. It was bought by the Duchy of Cornwall on behalf of the Prince. Highgrove includes a working farm, Home Farm, which sources many of the raw materials and ingredients used in the Prince's Duchy Originals products.

Separating public and private

There is considerable public confusion over exactly what constitutes the Queen's property and what is publicly owned. Vernon

Bogdanor has argued that it is impossible to distinguish between the private and public aspects of the monarch's life. For example, as the Queen carries out official functions from her private residences, they cannot be truly considered private and so should not be subject to tax.[10] However we find this argument unconvincing. The difference between the Crown Estate properties, which are held in trust for the nation, and those which belong privately to the Windsor family should be clear. Balmoral, Sandringham, Highgrove and the other private estates were bought with private funds and the royal family would be entitled to sell them if they chose to do so. Buckingham Palace, Windsor Castle and the other Crown palaces are forbidden to be sold by statute.

Consistent with earlier recommendations in this chapter, we believe that it is important to establish publicly a demarcation of this kind between the private property of the royal family and those properties which are effectively publicly owned and attached to the office of Head of State. To facilitate this a list of Crown property should be compiled and published in a similar way to the recent 'Domesday Book' exercise undertaken for government property by the Treasury. When publicly owned palaces fall empty, such as Clarence House did recently on the death of the Queen Mother, there should be proper public debate about how they are to be used, with proper accountability to public authority.

This is particularly important in relation to the sale of land. Since 1702 it has been illegal for any of the grounds of the royal homes – Kensington Palace, Buckingham Palace, St James's Palace and Windsor Castle – to be sold. However it was reported in 2002 that the Parliamentary agents Winckworth Sherwood had a private act passed in Parliament to enable the owners (Imperial Tobacco) of the Royal Garden Hotel in Kensington, London, dispensation to buy a plot of land owned by Kensington Palace. The *Guardian* reported:

'*The new legislation, under the title of Land at Palace Avenue, Kensington (Acquisition of Freehold) Act, got through Parliament virtually without debate in June. It gets round the thirty-one year lease by allowing Imperial Tobacco to start negotiating to buy a parcel of land.*

A spokesman for the department said yesterday [15 December 2002] "The money raised is expected to go to the Royal Household."' [11]

The laws on the sale of land owned by the monarch in right of the Crown and not personally need clarification. Even though legislation was passed to allow the sale of the land, there appears to have been very little public scrutiny of the decision. Moreover, given that the royal estates are held in trust for the nation, it is not clear why the proceeds went to the Royal Household. In future, where such land is sold, we believe that accounts should be presented to Parliament and the sums realised should be payable to the Treasury.

Along with the questions of ownership, issues have arisen in recent years about use. In particular attention has been drawn to the residential use of royal buildings at below market rents by members of the royal family and their staff. We believe there is too little transparency about who is being subsidised in this way and why. Again, the principle should be the separation of private and public. Working members of the royal family and their staff requiring subsidised accommodation should be publicly funded, with the money openly accounted for and under public scrutiny. If anyone else for whatever reason is given use of public property – and in principle public buildings should only be used in ways which meet public approval – market rents should be paid to the Crown Estate by the Queen or other members of the royal family out of private income, as the Queen is now doing for Prince and Princess Michael of Kent.

The public nature of Crown properties also needs, we believe, to be reflected in the degree of public access to them. The presumption should be that public properties are open to the public whenever possible – normally, unless there is good cause to the contrary, whenever they are not in residential use. The success of the public concerts at Buckingham Palace during the Golden Jubilee in 2002 suggests that grounds as well as buildings could be made more accessible, particularly for events.

The Royal Collection

In addition to land and buildings, the Crown owns substantial collections of art, jewellery and other artefacts. These are known as the Royal Collection. They include some of the world's most famous paintings with extraordinary historic and monetary value. As with the buildings their ownership status has been open to differing interpretation.

According to the Royal Collection Trust's annual reports, the collection is held by the Queen 'in right of the crown'. The Treasury's view is that the Crown Jewels, for example, are 'non-surrendered Crown property' which is 'vested in the sovereign and cannot be alienated.'[12] This interpretation is at odds, however, with the view given by the Duke of Edinburgh in a television interview in 2000. Speaking about some of the masterpieces in the Royal Collection, he noted that the Queen was, 'technically, perfectly at liberty to sell them'. The confusion is compounded by a statement by the then Lord Chamberlain, Lord Cobbold, to a Parliamentary Select Committee in 1971 in which he said that the Royal Collection is made up of items 'purchased or acquired by all sovereigns up to the death of Queen Victoria.' This seemed to imply that jewellery and art bought by or gifted to monarchs since 1901 are part of their private wealth.

One repercussion of the confused status of the Royal Collection is the inaccessibility to the public of information regarding its contents. For example, following the Windsor Castle fire in 1992, the public had no way of knowing for how much, or even if, the Royal Collection was insured; the official response of the Royal Collection Trust was that they never discussed such matters. This stands in stark contrast to information about the collections held by national museums, which is all fully in the public domain. With national museum collections the government has the final say over the fate of items of controversial provenance, such as the Parthenon Marbles in the British Museum. Yet it could not decide the fate of similarly controversial assets of the Crown, such as the Koh-i-Noor diamond.

Again it seems clear that there needs to be a clearer public distinction between those items that are the public property of the Crown, attached to the office of Head of State, and those that are the personal property of the sovereign and royal family. We welcome the ongoing work of the Royal Collection Trust, started in the 1980s, to create a publicly accessible inventory. This will help to clarify exactly which property belongs to the Crown thereby preventing confusion when minor pieces are sold off. For example, it was reported in December 2002 that two Gainsborough watercolours had been sold by a minor member of the royal family and replaced with high quality photographs of the paintings to disguise their sale. It appears that these were private pieces but an inventory would help to avoid such embarrassment in future. The inventory will emphasise the public nature of the collection; a planned website with pictures of the works will be particularly welcome.

Again we would strongly argue for the presumption that publicly owned art and artefacts should be publicly accessible. At present it is estimated that considerably less than one per cent of the Royal Collection can be seen by the public. This is, in our view, unacceptable. While there are clearly limits of space for exhibition, a much greater proportion should be available for public viewing at any time. This should include loans to museums and galleries, and to other public buildings such as town halls, hospitals and so on, throughout the country.

Gifts

The Royal Collection continues to grow, not least through the acquisition of gifts. The ownership and disposal of gifts attracted public attention in the wake of the Burrell affair in 2002, when it was revealed that the Prince of Wales's staff had received and sold gifts that may have properly been Crown property. The Peat Report, which investigated the affair, found that staff had indeed accepted and sold official gifts, in one case worth several thousand pounds. This was in clear breach of staff terms of employment, yet the report argued that this was not a matter for concern because the practice was tacitly approved by senior management at the Palace and the rules were not being enforced.[13]

It is extremely disturbing that there have not been absolutely clear guidelines on the status and use of gifts and that staff have been breaking terms of employment with regard to them. It is clear that such guidelines are needed and that they must be enforced, with clear disciplinary measures if breached. There need be no confusion as to the status of gifts. The Government set out the rules clearly in June 2002:

'Gifts are categorised as official [publicly owned] if given during an official engagement or in connection with the official role or duties of a member of the Royal Family.' [14]

Currently, records are kept of official gifts received by the Queen and of where they are stored. Other members of the royal family follow similar practice. Gifts received by any member of the royal family in a private capacity are not listed in official records. We believe that it would be helpful now if this system were open to public scrutiny. A public register on which members of the royal family would have to declare official gifts would prevent such gifts being sold privately and would enable genuinely private gifts to be treated separately.

Clearly there is a limit to the number of items that the Royal Collection can hold, and not every official gift will be retained. In such circumstances there should be no objection to the sale of gifts so long as the money raised goes towards public purposes, not into private hands. Further, such sales should be handled by an official curator, not by individual members of the royal family or their private staff.

Private income and wealth

Estimates of the Queen's wealth have often been greatly exaggerated as they mistakenly include items which are held by the Queen as Head of State on behalf of the nation and which are not her private property. As we have seen, these include most of the royal palaces, most of the art treasures from the Royal Collection, heirlooms in the Queen's jewellery collection and the Crown Jewels. Such 'inalienable' items held by the Queen as sovereign, rather than as an individual, cannot be disposed of and must pass to her successor.

Nevertheless it is almost certainly true that the Queen's private income, derived from her personal investment portfolio, is considerable. Most of the Queen's private investments are directed through a nominee company called the Bank of England Nominees. Many of the world's heads of state use the company to give them anonymity when buying shares. For this reason, when the Bank of England Nominees is listed as holding shares in a company, it is not possible to say who precisely is the true shareholder.

Therefore little is properly known about the detail of the Queen's personal wealth. The view of the Commission is that the private property and income of the monarch, as distinct from the public income and property of the Head of State, should be dealt with on the same basis as that of other citizens. This has particular relevance to the issue of taxation.

Taxation

Consideration of the income and wealth of the monarchy naturally leads to an examination of the taxation levied on the assets and the individuals involved. The present situation varies for different taxes. Indirect taxes on consumption, such as VAT, have always applied to the monarch. From most other taxes he or she has been exempt until relatively recently, with occasional longstanding voluntary arrangements such as over local rates and council tax.

The sovereign was notably exempt from taxes on income and wealth until 1992. In that year in a settlement negotiated with the then Prime Minister, John Major, the Queen offered to pay Income Tax and Capital Gains Tax on a voluntary basis. As from 1993 her personal income has therefore been taxable on the same basis as for any taxpayer. This includes the income received from the Privy Purse (the Duchy of Lancaster), subject to a deduction for official expenditure. From the same year the Prince of Wales has similarly paid tax on the income he receives from the Duchy of Cornwall, minus the expenditure incurred on public duties. The Civil List and the Grants-in-Aid are not remuneration for the Queen and are thus disregarded for tax.

In terms of Inheritance Tax the convention is that the monarch's estate is exempt so long as the transfer is made from sovereign to sovereign, that is, from the monarch to his or her successor. This was felt to give the monarch a degree of financial independence appropriate to constitutional impartiality. But the arrangements made in 1992 extended the rule to exempt bequests from the Queen Mother to the Queen, which were not made from sovereign to sovereign.

Council Tax is paid by all of the 244 residents of the royal palaces, including members of the Royal Family such as the Princess Royal and the Duke and Duchess of Kent. The Grant-in-Aid for property services is only responsible for Council Tax on vacant properties. Where a Crown dwelling is unoccupied, or occupied by the Queen or Prince Charles, a contribution is made in lieu of Council Tax, based upon the band which has been ascribed to it in the Valuation List.

As a crown body, the Duchy of Cornwall is tax exempt. However, since 1993 the Prince of Wales has voluntarily paid income tax (at the top rate of 40 per cent) on his income from the Duchy of Cornwall. The Prince had always paid a voluntary contribution to the Treasury. This was 50 per cent of his Duchy income from the time he became eligible for its full income at the age of 21 in 1969, and 25 per cent after his marriage in 1981. Tax is calculated after deducting business expenditure, the biggest source of which is the Prince's staff of around 80 (from private secretaries to valets) working in his office at St James's Palace and at his private residence of Highgrove.

The Commission's principle of the separation of the public and the private governs its approach to this subject. Where income is provided by the state to enable members of the royal family to carry out public duties it should not be taxed. Private income should be taxed on the same basis as that of other citizens. This should be a mandatory arrangement, not a voluntary one based only on goodwill.

Crown properties and the Royal Collection are public and should therefore not be subject to Inheritance Tax. Private properties and assets can be sold and should therefore be taxed on the same basis as they would be for other citizens. This includes both Capital Gains Tax and Inheritance Tax. The same exemptions should also apply. Where, for example, buildings and art works are accessible to the public they should not be subject to Inheritance Tax. These rules should include sovereign to sovereign bequests. Special exemptions, such as those made for the

Queen Mother, are not appropriate and should not be made in the future.

The same distinction between public and private already applies to gifts, as the Treasury has made clear.[15] Official gifts become public property and are not taxable; private gifts are personal property and are taxable.

Notes

1 *The Sunday Times*, Rich List 2003. Her personal wealth is currently estimated to be £250 million

2 'A queen's ransom' by Evan Davies, *Monarchies: What are Queens and Kings for?*, Tom Bentley and James Wilsdon (eds), Demos 2002

3 The *Guardian*, 28th June 2000

4 These comments are taken from Treasury files released in 2002, quoted in Alan Travis, 'Secret deals that obscure the royal finances', The Guardian, 30th May 2002

5 *ibid.*

6 *Office and Finance,* HRH The Prince of Wales, June 2003

7 *The Monarchy and the Constitution,* Vernon Bogdanor, Oxford 1995 p.194

8 *ibid.*

9 See www.royal.gov.uk

10 Bogdanor, *op. cit.* p.193'

11 Queen sells land at Kensington Palace' by David Hencke, The *Guardian*, 16th December 2002

12 Royal Collection Trust, Annual Report 2001-2002

13 *Report to His Royal Highness The Prince of Wales* by Sir Michael Peat and Edmund Lawson QC, March 2003

14 Answer given in Parliament by Gordon Brown, 24th June 2002

15 *ibid.*

Chapter 9

Conclusion and Summary of Recommendations

The UK has a deep and complex relationship with its monarchy. It is a relationship which has changed considerably over the fifty years since Queen Elizabeth II acceded to the throne, and, more particularly, over the last decade, during which the personal behaviour and largely private troubles of the royal family have attracted new levels of media attention. During these same periods British society has itself been changing dramatically, and the British constitution has been through its most significant period of reform for more than a century.

It was in this context that the Fabian Society established an independent Commission on the Future of the Monarchy in 2002. Comprising ten members with a range of experience and expertise, the Commission's aim was to consider the role and functions of the monarchy in a changing society and constitution, and to make recommendations on ways in which the office of Head of State 'could meet the social and political needs of today and the foreseeable future.'

Historically, the monarchy has provided Britain with an important symbol of continuity and stability. Yet at the same time it has constantly evolved to meet new social and constitutional circumstances. Representing for many a certain kind of historic British identity, and being associated with both pageantry and glamour on the one hand and notions of duty and service on the other, the monarchy has maintained a significant place in British life. It remains a remarkably popular institution at a time when other institutions have seen a marked decline in public confidence.

Yet the monarchy is more than a symbol; it is the centrepiece of Britain's constitution. Through all the recent constitutional changes and debates about them, from Scottish and Welsh devolution to the Human Rights Act, from reform of the House of Lords to abolition of the Lord Chancellor's office, there has been a curious silence about the institution at the summit of public life. The Fabian Commission's aim, therefore, was to define an appropriate constitutional and social role for the office of Head of State of the UK.

It was not, however, primarily to examine how the holder of that office should be appointed. So this report does not discuss the merits or otherwise of abolition of the monarchy or the creation of a republic. These issues should be debated; they are a vital part of the constitutional argument. But they were not our focus. Our aim was to define the office of a Head of State appropriate to modern Britain, whether that office was filled by a hereditary monarch or an elected president.

Principles for reform

In an abstract sense, the hereditary principle is not a good one. It would be unusual in the extreme to apply it to any new institution. Where it exists, such as in the House of Lords, there is widespread consensus against it. Yet in practice the UK's hereditary monarchy can be said to have several valuable characteristics. Its historical rootedness has served as a powerful source of 'social glue' in a country which has always been – and is now increasingly – characterised by geographic, ethnic and religious diversity and multiple identities. It provides continuity and a sense of historical stability in times of change. It is perceived to be above sectional and political interests. And it has widespread public support.

None of this however means that the monarchy should simply remain as it is. The Commission has come to the strong view that, if the institution is to survive in modern Britain, it needs reform. The risk it faces is that, unless it can become more representative at a symbolic level, and its functions more appropriate at a constitutional one, the strengths of the system will increasingly be undermined. The existence of a hereditary, unreformed apex to an otherwise democratic, pluralist state will come to look increasingly incongruous. The significant figures in opinion polls are perhaps not those supporting or opposing the monarchy's continued existence, but the numbers of people who believe that the monarchy matters and that its survival is important for Britain. These numbers have fallen markedly over recent years with particular falls among young people and in Scotland and Wales. The monarchy needs to continue its long process of historical evolution if it is to ensure its relevance in the Britain it serves.

Our argument is that the monarchy needs to become better adapted to the norms of contemporary British society and that its role within the systems of government and law need to be better defined. We believe that five principles should guide reform. These are:

Depoliticisation
The scope for political discretion should be removed from the duties and powers of the Head of State.

Separation of the public and private
There should be a clear demarcation between the public office of Head of State and the personal life and family affairs of its incumbent. In entirely personal affairs the Head of State, the heir and members of the wider royal family should as far as possible be on an equal footing with other citizens.

Representativeness
The office of Head of State should seek to represent Britain as it is and as it wishes to be, actively avoiding instances of discrimination and associating with all parts of Britain and British society.

Transparency
There should be full disclosure about the public business of the office of Head of State, including its finance and administration.

These should be subject to proper public scrutiny and accountability.

Professionalism
The office of Head of State should operate to the highest standards of professionalism, in keeping with the accepted norms of public office.

An agenda for reform

This report sets out an agenda for reform based on these principles. Its recommendations on reform to the constitutional powers and duties of the monarch as Head of State are designed to remove political discretion from the monarch's functions and to codify rules currently governed mainly by convention. Its recommendations on the rules of succession, on the relationship between the sovereign and the Church of England, on the public duties of the royal family and the staffing of the Royal Household, are all aimed at increasing the representativeness of the institution in relation to British society.

One of the consequences of a hereditary system is the blurring of the lines between the public institution of Head of State and the private life and family of the incumbent. The report argues that these lines need to be clearly drawn in areas such as the religious faith of the monarch, the composition and duties of the working royal family, the financing and administration of the Royal Household and the taxation of the sovereign and other family members. In all these areas, as befits a modern public institution, we argue that the affairs of the Head of State should be completely transparent and publicly accountable, and they should be run on a properly professional basis.

Succession
The symbolic nature of the monarchy as a unifier of the nation has long been important given the multinational character of the British state. However, Britain's longstanding national diversity, more pronounced now with devolution, is accompanied by increasing cultural diversity and an expectation of civil and

social equality. In these circumstances it should no longer be acceptable for the monarchy to embody what are effectively forms of institutionalised discrimination. We therefore recommend that the rules of succession should be reformed. Specifically:

- The line of succession should pass to the eldest child regardless of gender.
- The bar on Catholics in the Act of Settlement 1701 should be repealed, along with the requirement for the monarch to defend the Anglican faith. There should be no requirement for the British Head of State to hold any particular form of religious faith, or any faith at all.
- The Royal Marriages Act 1772, which forbids members of the royal family in line of succession from marrying without the consent of the monarch, should be repealed.
- Changes to the Accession Oath should be made to allow for the voluntary retirement of the monarch if he or she should so wish.

Constitutional powers and duties

The monarch's primary constitutional role is as Head of State. This is the near-universal office in modern constitutions, filled in different countries by election, appointment or birth. While in some states the office retains some degree of political discretion, this is inappropriate for a hereditary position in a democracy.

The current constitutional settlement in the UK leaves a number of residual powers with scope for political discretion in the hands of the monarch. By convention, these discretionary powers are rarely or never exercised, but the powers remain and could be used in different circumstances in the future. We argue that the scope for discretion on the part of the Head of State in the exercise of these powers and duties is not appropriate and should be removed. Specifically:

- The dissolution of Parliament should be regulated by statute. The Head of State should only be able to dissolve Parliament after five years, or on a majority vote in the House of

Commons. The Representation of People Act should be amended to specify a maximum interval of 6 weeks between the dissolution of Parliament and its summoning.

■ The appointment of the Prime Minister should be a matter for Parliament. The Head of State should recognise as Prime Minister whoever can command a majority in the House of Commons. The election of Prime Minister should be the first item for a new Parliament or in circumstances where no Prime Minister is in office, and the Speaker should manage the voting process. This should be codified in statute.

■ Royal assent to legislation should no longer include the possibility of discretionary action on the part of the Head of State. If not already given, the monarch's assent should be deemed to have been given after seven days.

Many of the powers nominally in the hands of the monarch as 'Royal Prerogative powers' are in fact exercised by Government ministers, notably by the Prime Minister, as executive powers unconstrained by the need to obtain parliamentary approval. The Commission regards these arrangements as unacceptable, for two reasons. First, they give unfettered powers to the executive in crucial areas, such as the declaration of war, which in most countries require parliamentary assent. Second, they misleadingly associate the exercise of these powers with the Head of State. We recommend:

■ All of the Prerogative powers currently exercised by the Executive should be put on a statutory basis with Parliament deciding, in passing the legislation, how those powers should be distributed and exercised. To reflect this, the term 'Royal Prerogative powers' should be abolished and replaced by the terms 'Parliamentary' and 'Executive' powers, depending on where they come to be located.

Alongside the monarch's constitutional powers and duties, the symbolism of the monarchy's place within the constitution is important. However, the present symbolic superiority of the unelected sovereign over the elected Parliament – in effect making Parliament an institution of the monarch rather than of the citizens – is no longer appropriate in a modern democracy. We argue therefore that:

- The State Opening of Parliament should take place only at the start of a new Parliament, not annually. The Queen's Speech should be replaced by an address by the Head of State relevant to the occasion of the opening of a new democratic Parliament. The legislative programme of the government should be presented by the Prime Minister at a separate parliamentary session and debated normally.
- The convention of the Humble Address, which requires Parliament to ask the monarch's permission before it can debate issues relating directly to him or her, should be removed, with a formal assertion of the right of Parliament to debate any issue.
- The current Oath of Allegiance, in which Members of Parliament and other public officials swear allegiance to the Crown, is inappropriate and in need of review. This review should seek a form of words that better reflects the public service commitment of those who take it.

The law

The position of a serving Head of State in relation to the law is problematic in most countries as completely equal treatment with other citizens is not possible. In the UK there are additional difficulties since in our unwritten constitution the monarch is regarded as the fount of law and therefore effectively above it. These complications must be recognised, but within them a greater degree of equal treatment is possible, and the symbolism of the monarch as above the law could be ended. Consequently we recommend:

- Immunities from claims in respect of civil offences committed by the monarch should be allowed. The ban on the criminal prosecution of serving heads of state is well established across the world and we do not recommend its removal.

- The Head of State should be competent to give evidence in court but no defendant should be able to compel him or her to stand as a witness.
- Prosecutions should be made in the name of the Director of Public Prosecutions rather than the Crown.

Religion

The British monarch holds a constitutional position in relation not only to the state, but also to the Church of England, of which he or she is Supreme Governor. This relationship is one element in the establishment of the Church of England. The monarch has a weaker relationship with the Church of Scotland. We do not believe that the close association between the Head of State and the Anglican Church is compatible with a Britain of diverse faiths and none. We argue that Church and state need to be distanced. At the same time the incumbent should be allowed to express his or her personal faith if desired.

In respect of the establishment of the Church of England, we recommend:

- The position of the Head of State as Supreme Governor of the Church of England should be ended.

This would in effect constitute a partial disestablishment of the Church of England. We regard the other elements of establishment, namely the appointment of bishops and their position in the House of Lords, and the parliamentary control of church legislation, to be matters respectively for the government in consideration of Lords reform and for the Church of England. They are not essentially matters relating to the position of Head of State. The universal geographic coverage of the Church of England would continue to make it the 'national church'. The constitutional relationship of the Head of State with the Church of Scotland should also be ended.

At present the ceremonies of both Coronation and Accession (when the new monarch formally accedes to the throne) are primarily religious. We recommend:

- The Accession Council should be seen as the point at which the Head of State takes up office, and should consequently be made secular, democratic and public. In the composition of those attending and in its ceremony it should be as representative of modern Britain as possible, and its symbolic focus should be on the democratic authority conferred on the monarch as Head of State. In the Accession Declaration or Oath the new Head of State should swear to serve the people of the UK and to uphold its constitution and laws.

- The precise character of the subsequent Coronation ceremony should remain flexible, as it has been in the past, to reflect the character of the times and the preferences of the incoming Head of State. As a blessing and celebration it could, but need not be, religious in character. The Coronation Oath itself, however, needs to be redrafted to be properly secular, again based on an undertaking to serve the people. The ceremony should seek to be representative of Britain in content and appearance.

The Commonwealth

The current position of the British monarch as Head of the Commonwealth of Nations is not a constitutional one. Established in 1948, there have only been two monarchs who have held the title. Over the last fifty years the position has become very strongly associated with Queen Elizabeth II personally, and it not clear that on her death it will be appropriate for her heir to accede to it. The nature and occupant of the role of Head of the Commonwealth is a matter for the member nations to determine. We recommend:

- The Commonwealth should be encouraged to make a decision about the future status of the office now, rather than waiting until a decision is required on the death of the Queen.

The Queen is Head of State of fifteen Commonwealth countries in addition to the UK. Any changes to the rules of succession of the British monarchy would therefore need to be agreed in consultation with those countries. However, since it is inconceivable that the UK should in any way interfere in the right of other sovereign states to choose their own Head of State, including those countries who currently have the Queen in that office, the UK could not allow other states to hold a right of veto over its own Head of State simply because they shared the same incumbent.

The royal family

In contrast to most other countries, including many constitutional monarchies, the UK's Head of State is surrounded by a wider group of family members who perform public functions. As well as the sovereign, her spouse and heir, 23 other members of the royal family receive state remuneration to perform public duties. Many of these duties are not integral to the functions of the Head of State. Yet they are valuable, and this aspect of the monarchy should not be abandoned carelessly.

There is nevertheless some public concern that too many peripheral members of the royal family receive public funds, in some cases in return for a rather small number of public duties. We argue that the definition of a 'working member of the royal family' should be reviewed and reformed:

- The number of members of the royal family in receipt of state funding should be limited to the monarch, his or her spouse, their offspring, and the children of the heir. Working members of the royal family would be able to continue in the role regardless of changes in family relationships, for example the death of the monarch.
- A member of the family who did not wish to perform public duties should be able to choose not to become a 'working royal'. Having 'opted out', they would have no further recourse to public remuneration or advantages.
- Being a 'working royal' – and consequently in receipt of state remuneration – should be seen as a serious job. It would involve undertaking an acceptable level of public duties and engagements and appropriate behaviour. 'Working royals' should not be allowed to participate in commercial activities.

Those who have opted out would be free to undertake any lawful business.

- The public engagements and roles undertaken by members of the royal family should be chosen to be representative of the nation as a whole. The royal family needs to associate itself with all parts of Britain, and with its many different social groups and activities, in order to be seen to reflect the nation they serve.

The Royal Household

The administration of the office of the Head of State currently blurs the distinction between the public and private aspects of the institution, with the 'Royal Household' including both the official and the domestic staffing of the monarch and heir. At the same time the existence of two, sometimes apparently rival, Palaces – Buckingham and St James's – has led to a lack of management coordination. Therefore we argue:

- The administration, staffing and financing of the public elements of the Royal Household should be completely separated from its private and domestic functions. It would be sensible to re-title the Royal Household the Office of the Head of State to mark a clear distinction between the public institution and the private affairs of its members.
- An externally recruited, professional Chief Executive should be appointed to Buckingham Palace to manage the Office of the Head of State. This post should have overall responsibility for the public duties of the royal family as a whole, and specifically for co-ordinating Buckingham and St James's Palaces. The Chief Executive should be the senior management position, working directly to the Head of State and able to act with his or her authority. The appointment should be openly advertised and made by the monarch on the advice of the Public Appointments Commission.
- The staff of the Office of the Head of State should be civil servants with the same status as those of other state departments, and with common recruitment procedures.

- An independent body of advisors should be appointed to advise on how the activities of the monarch and royal family can best serve the public and the country, particularly to ensure that the institution is, and looks, as representative as possible of the diversity of modern Britain.

Finance

The current arrangements for the financing of the monarchy are complicated and anomalous, with four separate public revenue streams: the Civil List, Grants-in-Aid, and the income from the Duchies of Lancaster (the Privy Purse) and Cornwall. Deriving from the historic unity of office and individual, they confuse the private income of the royal family with the public financing of the constitutional office of Head of State. We believe that reform is needed to bring proper clarity and accountability to the way the office of Head of State is financed:

- All aspects of finance for the Head of State, the heir and working members of the royal family should be combined into a single, transparent and accountable public revenue stream, subject to a vote in Parliament. This would combine the current Civil List with the Privy Purse, the Grants-in-Aid and, in the case of the Prince of Wales, the income from the Duchy of Cornwall.
- The titles to the Crown Estate and to the Duchies of Lancaster and Cornwall, currently held by the sovereign and heir in trust, should be formally transferred to the nation, to be managed by the Crown Estates Commissioners. The land of the Duchies, the royal palaces and so on should continue to be held in trust for the nation.
- Public annual reports of the finances of the office of Head of State should be required to be presented to Parliament in a comprehensive and readily understandable form.

Property

There needs to be a clear demarcation between those lands, buildings, artworks and other assets which are the private property of the royal family and those which belong to the nation. Consequently:

- A public register of Crown property owned by the nation should be compiled in a similar way to that undertaken for Government property by the Treasury. A similar inventory of the Royal Collection of art is already being compiled.
- There should be a general presumption that land, buildings and art which belong to the nation should be publicly accessible. Properties should be opened up wherever possible when not in use, and a much greater proportion of the art in the Royal Collection should be available for public viewing at any time. This should include loans to museums and galleries and other public buildings throughout the country.

Crown assets belong to the nation. Therefore they should not be disposed of or used simply in accordance with the personal decisions or for the personal gain of members of the royal family. Consequently:

- The public subsidy of rents on residential property owned by the Crown is acceptable only where required for working members of the royal family and their staff. Such subsidies must be completely transparent. Any other residential use should be at market rents and repaid to the Crown Estate out of the private funds of the monarch or heir.
- The laws on the sale of land owned by the Crown need clarification. Where land is sold there should be public scrutiny and accountability. The profits should go to the Crown.
- Clear guidelines relating to gifts made to members of the royal family need to be established and enforced in line with the recommendations of the Peat Report in 2003.
- A public register of official gifts should be established. Any sales of gifts should be undertaken only by an official curator, with the money going to public purposes.

Taxation

The lack of clarity between the public and private aspects of the monarchy is reflected in the tax arrangements of the monarch and heir. Both present incumbents have made voluntary arrangements to pay income tax, but such matters should not be a matter of goodwill. We recommend:

- The Head of State and all other members of the royal family should pay tax on their private income and wealth in line with the taxation rules for other private individuals.
- Properties and assets owned privately by the monarch and other members of the Royal Family (such as the Balmoral, Sandringham and Highgrove estates) should be subject to both Capital Gains Tax and Inheritance Tax on the same basis as they would be for other citizens. These rules should include sovereign to sovereign bequests. But normal exemptions should also apply so that where, for example, buildings and art works are accessible to the public they would not be subject to Inheritance Tax. Crown properties and the Royal Collections are publicly owned and should therefore not be subject to tax.

Implementing reform

We have proposed a number of reforms to the institution of the monarchy as it is currently organised. But we do not suggest that the implementation of these reform should be achieved through a single, unified package of measures.

Some recommendations could clearly be taken up as internal matters by the Palaces themselves, such as our proposals on management structure and staffing policies and our suggestions on how the public duties of the royal family could be changed to ensure that they are representative of modern Britain. Others require specific regulation or amendment to existing legislation, such as changes to the Representation of the People Act in respect of the summoning of Parliament. Some could be implemented immediately; others would take longer.

Where legislation is needed, a piecemeal approach to reform, mixed with regulation where appropriate, would be more in keeping with the historically evolved nature of the UK constitution than a single portmanteau Act of Parliament. Being lower key in character it would also perhaps offer fewer political risks for a government keen on reform but concerned about the context of public opinion. It may also make for an easier relationship of collaboration with the institutions of the monarchy itself.

We do however believe that some of our proposed reforms would require significant acts of legislation, notably those codifying the constitutional powers and duties of the Head of State and reforms to the rules of succession. These reforms we believe should be contained in two new Acts of Parliament.

The first, a Succession Act, should in part replace the Act of Settlement 1701 in setting out the new rules of succession. Second, a Constitution Act should define the scope and exercise of the powers of the Head of State. This should reform the use of Royal Prerogative powers, both those (such as Royal Assent to legislation) currently exercised by the monarch, and those now exercised by ministers. The Act should also define and limit the extent of the Head of State's immunities in relation to the law.

We recognise that the Government may regard some of our proposed reforms as politically difficult. The reluctance of ministers to address these issues is understandable given the extent of popular support for the monarchy and the other demands on legislative time. Yet the evidence suggests that public opinion, still firmly behind the institution itself, is open to the idea of change. Just as importantly, there are strong indications that the Palaces themselves are willing to countenance reform. As the Queen observed in her address to Parliament in 2002, the historic strength of the monarchy has been its ability to adapt to changed circumstances. We believe that the lessons of the turbulent events of recent years – both the successes, such as the Golden Jubilee, and the troubles, such as the Burrell trial – point in the direction of reform set out by this report.

Since 1997 the present Government has embarked on an ambitious programme of constitutional reform. From Scottish and Welsh devolution through the Human Rights Act to the proposed abolition of the Lord Chancellor's office, most of the key institutions in our system of governance have been addressed. At the same time the Government has sought to reflect the new and diverse Britain of the twenty-first century. We believe there is a strong case now for the reform programme to include the institution so central to the British constitution and to British society.

Terms of Reference and Members of the Commission

Terms of Reference

The Commission examined the role and functions of the monarchy and its position within a changing society and constitution. It was asked to make recommendations on ways in which the office of Head of State can meet the social and political needs of today and the foreseeable future.

The Commission considered, *inter alia*, the following issues:

- The role, duties and powers of the monarch in the British constitution.
- The role played by the monarchy and the royal family in British history, society and economy, and in different conceptions of national identity and citizenship.
- The principles which should guide any constitutional reform to the office of Head

of State and its relationships with the office of Prime Minister, Government, Parliament and other local, national and supranational institutions.

- The principles which should guide any reforms to the other relationships between the monarch and the state and possible options for such reform - in areas such as the Civil List, taxation, property and the law.
- The relationship between the Head of State and the Church of England.
- The impact of such reform on Commonwealth countries for whom the monarch is also Head of State, and on the Commonwealth itself.

Method of Working

The Commission met regularly from May 2002 to January 2003. Drawn from the Terms of

Reference, specific questions were considered, with oral evidence being taken from expert witnesses. In addition, written evidence was taken from a variety of sources. The topics considered and witnesses called were agreed by the Commission during its deliberations.

Membership

The Commission comprised the following members:

- Chair: David Bean QC, barrister
- Lord Waheed Alli, television production entrepreneur and Labour peer
- Sir Michael Wheeler-Booth, former Clerk of the Parliaments and member of the Royal Commission on the House of Lords
- Andrew Gamble, Professor of Politics at Sheffield University and Co-Editor of the *Political Quarterly*
- Claude Moraes MEP and former Director of the Joint Council for the Welfare of Immigrants
- Professor Kenneth Morgan (Lord Morgan of Aberdyfi), historian and former Vice-Chancellor of the University of Wales, Aberystwyth

- Dawn Oliver, Professor of Constitutional Law at University College London
- Alison Park, Research Director at the National Centre for Social Research
- Paul Richards, Chair of the Fabian Society
- Mary Riddell, author and columnist on the *Observer* and the *Daily Mail*

Secretary to the Commission: Adrian Harvey, Deputy General Secretary of the Fabian Society

Secretariat support for the Commission was provided by the Fabian Society

Evidence to the Commission

Witnesses who appeared in person

- Anthony Barnett, Editor, OpenDemocracy and writer on constitutional issues
- Robert Blackburn, Professor of Constitutional Law, King's College London
- Vernon Bogdanor, Professor of Government at the University of Oxford
- Rt Rev Colin Buchanan, Bishop of Woolwich
- Linda Colley, Professor of History and Leverhulme Research Professor, LSE
- Evan Davies, economist
- Stephen Haseler, Chair of Republic – the Campaign for an elected Head of State
- David McCrone, University of Edinburgh
- Bhikhu Parekh, Chair of the Commission on the Future of Multi-Ethnic Britain
- Shridath Ramphal, former Secretary General of the Commonwealth

- Penny Russell-Smith, Press Secretary to The Queen, Buckingham Palace
- Simon Walker, former Communications Secretary, Buckingham Palace
- John Williams, Menzies Centre for Australian Studies, King's College London

Written evidence

- Richard Bourne, Institute of Commonwealth Studies
- Michael Hyde, Suffolk Fabian Society
- Geoffrey Marshall, constitutional theorist
- David Metz, London School of Hygiene and Tropical Medicine
- Kevin McNamara MP
- Sir Michael Peat, Private Secretary to the Prince of Wales, St James's Palace
- Brian Selway QC, Menzies Centre for Australian Studies, King's College London

Note by Sir Michael Wheeler-Booth

Part I

I was asked to join the Commission as a non-party student of the constitution, with an interest in recent changes in our institutions, but I had not studied the monarchy in any depth before. Attendance at the Commission and consideration of the evidence collected by the enquiry have convinced me that radical reform of the monarchy would be inappropriate. Part I of this note gives my conclusions. Part II gives instances of where I regretfully differ from the Commission report, and Part III enumerates those proposals for moderate evolutionary reform which I agree should be considered.

This country has undergone much constitutional reform in recent years. As Bagehot noted long ago, 'A new Constitution does not pro-duce its full effect as long as all its subjects were reared under an old Constitution.' Time is now needed to allow the recent changes to settle. A period of consolidation is required, except where it can be shown that further changes are absolutely necessary. In the case of the monarchy, there are many reasons why no major changes are required, and that for the moment – after the excitements of the Jubilee – 'a period of silence' would be wise.

As an island nation, we have been fortunate not to have suffered successful invasion or face the need for complete constitutional renewal, as was the case in America after 1776, or in Germany in 1947. Rather we possess an old institution which has slowly evolved over the centuries into a democratic constitutional monarchy. As my colleagues note, a country is foolish to ignore its history or the emotional strings which bind us to it. The monarchy is one of the strongest of our institutions and is the continuing living embodiment of our past. Shakespeare articulated this sentiment in an earlier age, and Churchill more recently at our time of peril in 1940.

The monarchy evidently remains popular. This reflects the good sense of the electorate, who distinguish between the human frailties within the royal family and the underlying unifying force reflected in the life and work of the Queen. Contrary to the interests of elements in the media, it is not publicity which the monarchy requires, but rather a period of calm and to be left alone.

We are fortunate to have a system whereby the position of Head of State is beyond the reach of the political parties. At a time when there is disillusion with the political process and electoral turnout is low, this is a benefit to the electorate and indeed to the political parties and government. It was for this reason that in the recent referendum in Australia the republican option was rejected. The electorate was suspicious of a constitutional change that would have increased the role of the salaried elected party politician.

Part II
I regret having to dissent from my colleagues, but this has resulted from the radical nature of some of their suggested changes, based on evidence which has failed to convince me. In particular I dissent from the reforms in relation to the Queen's formal powers. Changes involving legislation should be avoided unless necessary. It is inconceivable that the Queen would refuse her assent to a bill duly passed by the two Houses, unless on advice from ministers, who would only do so if major fault had been found in proposed legislation at the last moment. The changes proposed in the report in the relationship between the monarchy and the Church of England would raise complex issues and should only be undertaken at the request of the Church, and after careful consideration. In the light of these com-

plexities, I do not believe that the Commission gave this question sufficient examination to justify its recommendation.

I support however the Commission's recommendations of reform to the way in which the Royal Prerogative is used by the government as a cloak for executive action, without prior parliamentary consent. The recent choice taken to submit the decision whether to go to war with Iraq to debate and vote in the Commons was a significant evolutionary reform of the relationship between the executive and Parliament. Restrictions of existing practice in the use of the Royal Prerogative would be welcome and would represent an extension of democratic parliamentary powers at the expense of ministers and departments.

The Government has carried through wide constitutional changes - the most significant for many years. All its 1997 manifesto commitments have been put into effect, except electoral reform for the Commons and phase two of Lords reform. In that manifesto they wisely pledged 'we have no plans to replace the monarchy'. That remains the Government's policy.

Part III

For the above reasons, large changes in the role of the monarchy are undesirable. But this is not to say that limited piecemeal reforms should not be considered over a period, after appropriate consultations with the Queen, Parliament, government and public (in each case considering, where legislation would be required, whether the time and effort would be justified). I would include all of the following recommendations made by the Commission:

- *Oath of Allegiance*
  The forms of the Oaths of Allegiance taken in Parliament and elsewhere might be reviewed.
- *Rules of Succession*
  The existing rule for the Sucession to the Crown might be simplified to remove the provisions whereby male heirs enjoy precedence over females. This would be

easy to do now with three male heirs.

- *Royal Marriages Act 1772*
  This Act is redundant, and requires to be replaced by a simpler measure to apply to those few in the immediate line of succession.
- *Act of Settlement 1700*
  When the present conflicts in Northern Ireland allow, the provisions of this Act (and related Acts) prohibiting the sovereign or his consort from being a Roman Catholic should be considered, with a view to repeal.
- *Royal Prerogative*
  The use of the Royal Prerogative by the government without prior parliamentary consent should be reviewed.
- *Royal Finances*
  There is a case for simplifying and making more transparent the royal accounts, and making their administration more accountable. Measures should be taken to make the royal works of art and palaces more accessible.
- *Royal Household*
  Consideration should be given to the creation of a unified Royal service, under the Queen's Private Secretary (recruited with the help of the Civil Service Commission), to serve the Queen and others in the royal family.
- *Royal Family*
  The existing definition of the royal family, laid down by George V in 1917 by Royal Warrant, should be amended to redefine and restrict its membership, and to permit voluntary renunciation of the role.
- *Royal Ceremonies and Protocol*
  As the Queen has already indicated, royal ceremonies and protocol should evolve, if that is the popular wish, in such a way to combine and preserve the best of historic ceremonial with its trans-Britannic symbolism with gradual changes in keeping with the modern age.

One of the foremost characteristics of our monarchy has been its willingness to embrace gradual change, and this should continue to be the objective for the new century.